tate

THE ART MAGAZINE

ISSUE Nº 17
SPRING 1999

KU-735-650

Art elevated and grounded. From the top: Rachel Whiteread, 'Water Tower', 1998; William Dobson, 'Portrait of Charles 1', c.1635; Richard Deacon, 'Art for Other People 41', 1997. Cover: Jackson Pollock in his studio standing in front of 'Number 32', 1950

CONTRIBUTORS

Kathleen Adler is head of education at the National Gallery

Lewis Biggs is the director of Tate Gallery Liverpool

Andrew Brighton is a critic and curator, and head of public events at the Tate Gallery

Ian Davenport is an artist

Helen Frankenthaler is an artist

James Hall is a writer. His book, *The World as Sculpture: the changing status of sculpture from the Renaissance to the present day*, is published shortly by Chatto and Windus

Callum Innes is an artist. His exhibition at the Kunsthalle, Bern, runs until 28 March

Waldemar Januszczak is art critic of the *Sunday Times* and recent presenter of *The Truth about Art* on Channel 4

Michael Leja is associate professor of art history at the Massachusetts Institute of Technology and author of *Reframing Abstract Expressionism*, Yale University Press

Jeremy Lewison is director of collections at the Tate Gallery

Martin Maloney is an artist, curator

and writer and is showing in "Neurotic Realism" at the Saatchi Gallery

Jeremy Millar is an artist and programme organiser at the Photographers' Gallery. He curated "Speed" at the Whitechapel Art Gallery and the Photographers' Gallery, and is the editor, with Michiel Schwarz, of *Speed – Visions of an Accelerated Age*

Stephen Polcari is the former director of the Smithsonian Institution Archives of American Art in New York and author of *Abstract Expressionists and*

the Modern Experience, published by Cambridge University Press

Irit Rogoff is professor of visual culture at Goldsmiths and author of *Terra Infirma – Geography's Visual Culture*, published by Routledge

Julian Schnabel is an artist. His recent work is on show at the South London Gallery until 28 February

Rory Snookes is a painter and writer currently working on a PhD on Bacon

David Sylvester is an art critic and curator. He has just completed a monograph on Francis Bacon

PETER GWYTHER GALLERY

Peter Blake with *Babe Rainbow*

PETER BLAKE & ANDY WARHOL
PRINTS

22 January - 27 Febuary

PETER GWYTHER GALLERY
29 Bruton Street
London W1X 7DB

Tel 0171 495 4747
Fax 0171 495 6232
Cambart@aol.com

Editorial

Editor Tim Marlow
Art Director Stephen Coates
Production Editor Ian Massey
Assistant Editor Jessica Lack
Contributing Editors Charlotte Mullins, Simon Grant
Picture Researcher Juliet Duff
Interns Robert Wilson, Hester Westley

Publishing Director Nick Barley
Deputy Publisher Miranda Dunbar-Johnson
Assistant Publisher Philip Allison
Production Manager Nicola Vanstone
Production Co-ordinator Eva Wolpert
Membership Co-ordinator Julia Diamantis
Retail Co-ordinator Christopher Coombes

Thanks and acknowledgements
Simon Wilson, Emma Rhind-Tutt, Damien Whitmore, Kate Burvill, Ina Cole, Catherine Braithwaite, Tiffany Vignoles, Rachel Oglethorpe, Ben Luke, Rachel Whiteread, Richard Deacon, Chris Burden, Micheline Phankim, Graham Leggat, Jessica Ferraro, Pepe Karmel

Aspen Publishing
Avon House, Kensington Village
Avonmore Road, London W14 8TS
Telephone 0171 906 2002
Fax 0171 906 2004

Published by Aspen Publishing in association with the Tate Gallery
Copyright © 1999

No responsibility can be accepted for unsolicited manuscripts or photographs
ISSN 1351-3737

Printing St Ives (Roche) Ltd
Colour reproduction DawkinsColour
Newstrade distribution Comag Specialist Division, Mercury Centre, Central Way, Feltham, Middlesex TW14 0RX
Bookshop distribution Central Books, 99 Wallis Road, London E9 5LN
Subscriptions *tate* subscriptions, Galleon, Building 960 Sittingborne Research Centre, Kent ME9 8AG.
tel 01795 414 500
USA subscriptions *tate*, PO Box 1584, Birmingham, AL 35201-1584
Toll free number: 1-800-633-4931
tate is published by Aspen Publishing Subscription price is US$29.
Send USA address corrections to:
tate, c/o Mercury Airfreight International Inc, Falcon House Central Way, Feltham, Middlesex TW14 0UQ

tate is the art magazine with an international perspective, which emerges from a close relationship with the Tate Gallery and reflects the expanding role of the gallery in the contemporary cultural debate. It is, however, an independent publication, with its own voice and vision

I can't remember ever being quite so excited at the prospect of an exhibition coming to London as I am about the Pollock retrospective. It was stunning in New York where it opened at the Museum of Modern Art last November and both the critical and public reaction to the show was phenomenal. New York, though, was Pollock's adopted city and it has the largest and most important collection of the painter's work in the world. Britain, on the other hand, has few Pollocks and fewer masterpieces and has not staged a significant Pollock show for 40 years, let alone the largest exhibition of the artist's work ever assembled.

Off hand, I can't think of any major twentieth-century artist who has been seen so infrequently, and Pollock is clearly not only a major figure in the art of the past hundred years, he's also the pivotal figure in post-war painting: the artist described by fellow Abstract Expressionist Willem de Kooning as the man who "broke the ice" and who developed a radical new way of painting, the implications of which are still not fully grasped, even today.

At least two generations of gallery goers and, more crucially, artists will never have seen a substantial amount of Pollock's painting, nor have been able to see, at first hand, how vital, sensual, violent, lyrical, poetic, dense, disturbing, refined, liberated and complex it really is.

Consequently, it's not hard to predict the impact that the current exhibition will have, not just on painting, but on art in general in Britain in the next few years – establishing, as it does, Pollock's credentials as an old master in the making and a contemporary artist whose work still seems fresh, relevant, difficult and breath-taking. Enjoy the experience.
Tim Marlow

Hans Namuth's photograph of Jackson Pollock in his East Hampton studio, autumn, 1950

© 1999 HANS NAMUTH LTD

TEFAF MAASTRICHT

1999

Information:
The European
Fine Art Foundation
+31 73 614 51 65
http://www.tefaf.com

**International Fine Art
and Antiques Fair**

**13 – 21 March 1999
MECC Maastricht
The Netherlands**

**TEFAF Basel 1999
13 – 21 November**

Upfront

CONTRIBUTORS
DAVID BARRETT, ANGELO CAPASSO,
ALEXA DE FERRANTI, ROSIE DE LISLE,
JOSEPH HOUSEAL, RICHARD INGLEBY,
IMOGEN O'RORKE, JOE QUIGG, RUTH
ROSENGARTEN, MATS STJERNSTEDT,
NAOMI STUNGO, ROB WILSON
COMMISSIONING EDITORS: SIMON GRANT
AND JESSICA LACK

Still modern after all these years...

New York is basking in post-Ab-Ex bliss after MoMA's epic Pollock show and the Whitney's smaller, but equally intense, Rothko exhibition. In addition, Larry Gagosian staged a beautiful Gorky show and the increasingly important Drawings Center downtown in SoHo invited Klaus Kertess to select 70 rarely seen drawings by Willem de Kooning which are currently touring the States (Addison Gallery in Andover, Mass, until 28 March, Wexner Center, Ohio State University, 15 May-15 August).

Having reasserted the ongoing power of the New York School, the city now prepares to promote the whole of twentieth-century American art in a vast two-part, 1,600-strong extravaganza at the Whitney beginning in April, with part two following in September. "The American Century: Art and Culture, 1900-2000" boldly goes where few have dared to follow, namely in the curatorial footsteps of Norman Rosenthal and Christos Joachamedes, whose "American Art in the Twentieth Century" in Berlin and at the Royal Academy (with a postscript at the Saatchi Gallery) in 1993 proved conspicuously underwhelming. Hopes are higher for a multi-disciplinary show featuring architecture, music, dance, literature and film, as well as painting, sculpture and photography.

Meanwhile, aside from the celebration and promotion of American culture, the Museum of Modern Art is still wrestling with its own cultural identity having just lost four post-Impressionist drawings bequeathed by founder Abby Rockefeller on the grounds that they are no longer modern. In her will, written in 1947, Rockefeller stipulated that two

Charcoal and oil drawing by Willem de Kooning, 1970-1979

drawings by Van Gogh and two by Seurat should leave MoMA after 50 years, with the former going through Central Park to the Met and the latter winging their way to the Chicago Institute of Art to be reunited with Seurat's epic 'Sunday Afternoon at La Grande Jatte', for which they are studies. MoMA director Glen Lowry observed that "had Abby Rockefeller been alive today it is unlikely she would have given the drawings to the Met" on the grounds that "both MoMA and the Met had radically changed" since the 1940s. Faced, however, with a legal *fait accompli*, Lowry was bullish, adding that "the Modern has consistently changed its ideas as its place in history has changed dramatically, and it will continue to do so".

At the Chicago Museum of Contemporary Art, it's not so much works of art that are leaving as directors. Kevin Consey departed before Christmas and has been replaced by Robert Fitzpatrick, who brings the established (California Institute of the Arts) along with the "my-God-that's-American" to the directorial hot seat. Fitzpatrick was formerly president of Euro-Disney and vice-president of the Los Angeles 1984 Olympics Arts Festival. Remember, that was the only Olympics in history with a colour scheme. The windy city awaits the hitherto unannounced roster of events. It had better be hip.

What's new in the US might be understood as what's new to the US with the Art Institute of Chicago staging three major exhibitions, each of which consists largely of works never before seen on our "uncultured but revolutionary soil" (hello Ben Franklin). The first of these, "Masterpieces from Central Africa: Selections from the Belgian Royal Museum for Central Africa, Tervuren" (until 14 March) continues the Institute's legacy of presenting non-western art within its embracing context of new western scholarship and esteem.

More in line with its legendary late-nineteenth-century French exhibitions come 175 works by Gustave Moreau (13 February-25 April). While certainly there's the millennial need to see past centuries' millennial expressions, this show may be more useful – shedding light on Moreau's student Matisse and his Belgian protégé Magritte. Indeed, Moreau emerges as both über-symbolist and proto-surrealist where art slips comfortably into bed with literature.

Elsewhere along the Magnificent Mile, the Arts Club of Chicago retains its unique policy of presenting a series of contemporary artists. Try out the white marble works and bronze and painted sculpture of Saint Clair Cemin (18 February-3 April), whose work, to quote the critic Charles Merewether, "is a constant detour, of reason and folly, of perception and memory, of logic and desire, of life and death". So, if you want to know what Proust would be in sculpture... *JH & JQ*

The realisation of dreams

At another moment in time the city of Dundee might have made a claim for the Keiller collection: it was at one time, after all, the golf-playing marmalade heiress's adopted town. But in these days of public partnerships and Lottery funding all available cash has gone into a new arts centre on the banks of the Tay.

Dundee Contemporary Arts opens on 20 March. Director Andrew Nairne, formerly of the Scottish Arts Council and the Third Eye Centre in Glasgow, sees it as a centre for everyone "rooted in the life of the city and engaged with and open to the world". The opening show includes Warhol, Beuys and Catherine Yass (her piece, 'Bridge: East', is pictured right) alongside the more local talents of Callum Innes and Louise Hopkins. Nairne seems to have a genuine belief that anything is possible. Time will tell whether the reality can match the dream, but, on paper at least, DCA looks like an inspirational model for the new millennium. *RI*

Jane and Louise Wilson

Twins peek

The creation of spooky, hammy horror movie atmospheres to stir the subconscious and rouse unwanted memory from the deep, is what Jane and Louise Wilson (pictured right) do best. It was their 'Hypnotic Suggestion 505', shown at the "British Art Show 4" in 1995, which triggered off media interest in their act. A video sequence in which, dressed and groomed identically, the twins respond simultaneously to the spoken commands of a hypnotist, the piece was about our compliance in mass auto-suggestion through the medium of cinema, but it said more about the sisters' strange synchronistic relationship.

Much was made of their telepathic talents at the time: they both came up with identical final year shows, despite going to different art colleges, Jane to Newcastle, Louise to Dundee. The Wilsons have since tried to defuse the coincidence ("It was simply the evidence that persuaded us we should be working together," says Jane), but there is no doubt that their early work, 'Normapaths' (1995) and 'Crawl Space' (1995) – a pastiche of all their favourite horror movie moments from *The Exorcist* to *Carrie* and *Twin*

Jane and Louise Wilson, 'Normapaths', 1995

Peaks – is predicated on their relationship as colluders, plotters, crazy siblings "off on their own trip".

Then, just as the YBA press sensation was hotting up in 1996, the Wilsons disappeared off to Germany on a DAAD scholarship and missed out on their share of the limelight. Two years on, they are very much back on the British scene, this time storming the old American base on Greenham Common in search of a good location for their latest show at the Lisson Gallery (18 February–1 April). It follows on from their 'Stasi City', which has been shown throughout Germany and in New York. 'Stasi City' was shot at the

former headquarters of East German intelligence in two days with very little preparation, taking in images of empty corridors and interrogation rooms – all unchanged since the day the Wall came down. The split-screen installation had a chilling, schizophrenic air. The Wilsons themselves appeared only as props, a leg dangling here, an unidentified floating body there. "We wanted to make work which was relevant to Germany," says Jane.

The Greenham Common project, 'Gamma', is a similar undertaking. "We are interested in documenting architectural phenomena, abandoned bureaucratic buildings, buildings where there is a pathology attached" (Jane). "Buildings which are hidden from the public eye, which are not

Jane and Louise Wilson, 'Gamma', an installation work in progress: hangar 303 (top) and the command centre communication room at Greenham Common, 1998

easy to access" (Louise). After weeks of petitioning the MoD, they were finally granted two unofficial visits to the site. Their studio at Delfina, in the meantime, has turned into a temporary spy base, plastered with photographs of Greenham and a sunken airbase in Epping. The documentation in itself is very powerful, reminding you how good they are at photography.

The aftermath of the Cold War, the lingering pathology of the nuclear threat, is all too present in, for example, the decontamination chamber marked with arrows to guide the contaminated through and the echoing silos where the warheads were kept near hangar 303. Most Wilsonesque (via Kubrick, De Palma and Tarkovsky) are the images of the dormitories where the US soldiers lived, decorated with strange medallions of eagles and bulldogs, put there, you presume, to make the soldiers seem more at home.

Being dedicated CND supporters throughout their teenage years, the Wilsons have chosen subject matter which is close to home. It will be interesting to see how they will incorporate themselves into the film, if at all. *IO'R*

SWEDEN

The elegaic great outdoors

The young Danish artist Olafur Eliasson (due to make his UK debut at Dundee Contemporary Arts in September) is one of a growing number of Scandinavians to take up Robert Smithson's elegaic inquiry into form and space in the glorious outdoors.

Good news it is then, that a touring show of Smithson's work is now set in stone. Beginning at the National Museum of Contemporary Art, Oslo (27 February-2 May), it's a comprehensive collection, including preparatory material for wondrous works such as 'Spiral Jetty', that will no doubt generate a platform for a timely reassessment of his work. As Scandinavian artists increasingly look for influences from international sources (a welcome shift away from the quasi-nationalistic art of the 1980s), Smithson should hit the mark.

It may be a coincidence, but the season is characterised by exhibitions by American artists. One of these is Chris Burden, showing three works in the sparkling, refurbished public space,

A view of "Cities on the Move 4" showing work by Heri Dono and Pasti Boleh

Magasin 3, in Stockholm (6 February-5 May, and also at the Tate Gallery, 16 February-6 June). As with the Tate project, he continues his exploratory studies into time and motion. Like Smithson, Burden is an increasingly influential figure in Scandinavia, so this show (two works from the 1970s, plus a commissioned piece) should attract a good audience.

The Moderna Museet's spring programme includes "Neue Welt" (27 March-9 May), showcasing recent

work by the arch-sociologist and ex-scientist Carsten Höller. Always a man to have a bit of fun with his art, the exhibition looks at our need for competition and game play. Not that the art world needs that kind of scrutiny, of course. Höller's work often enjoys the potential for audience participation, so visitors should remember to go with the right attitude and a belief that you, too, can change the world.

The Louisiana Museum of Modern Art at Humlebæk, near Copenhagen, takes on "Cities on the Move 4" (until 21 April), a touring show curated by the prolific Hans-Ulrich Obrist along with Hou Hanru. One hundred artists and architects focus on the intensive cultural life found in today's Asian cities, while a couple of working tuk-tuks may be on hand to transport visitors around town, Asian style. Keen to maintain a flexible curatorial approach, Obrist and Hanru have asked Japanese artist Tsuyoshi Osawa to make a show within a show. Osawa has created a temporary gallery made from a series of painted blue birdhouses, within which ten artists each display a piece of work. Who said curators did all the hard work? "Cities on the Move 4" tours to the Hayward Gallery (13 May-27 June) and then to the Finnish National Museum of Contemporary Art in Helsinki. *MS*

Russian roulette

Kasimir Malevich, the pioneering, hard core abstract painter and champion of the avant-garde in Russia in the early twentieth century, was asked to build a collection of work for a new Museum of Fine Art Culture. Designed to reflect the spirit of optimism and radical artistic achievements of the years leading up to and into the Revolution, Malevich began amassing works in 1918, stopping when it was announced in 1926 that plans for the museum would not go ahead. Instead, the collection was installed in the State Russian Museum in St Petersburg, from which the Barbican Art Gallery has put together "New Art for a New Era: Malevich's Vision of the Russian Avant-Garde" (29 April-27 June), a selection of more than 80 pieces with work by Marc Chagall, Matharie Goncharova, Wassily Kandinsky, Aleksandr Rodchenko, Vladimir Tatlin (his 'Sailor', 1911, is pictured left) and Malevich himself. *AdeF*

GERMANY

Station to station

Martin Kippenberger, who died last year at the age of 44, mythologised himself through his work, creating a kind of anti-hero persona. No surprise, then, that many works were self-portraits. You can see some of them at Deichtorhallen in Hamburg (11 February–25 April). About 130 self-portrait drawings travel from their recent showing at the Kunsthalle Basel to team up with paintings from a private collection, as well as the Louisiana Museum's 'The Happy End of Franz Kafka's "Amerika" ' – a large-scale furniture installation. The exhibition also features many of his 'Hotel Drawings', executed on the headed notepaper of various hotels worldwide to form a sardonic diary of his life as one of the international homeless.

Bill Viola was largely responsible for helping video art out of its technological niche. It is remarkable that he has been working for 25 years, as an important retrospective testifies (at no fewer than seven sites around Frankfurt). "Bill Viola: 25 Year Survey" tours from the US and is showing at the Museum für Moderne Kunst (until 25 April) and the Schirn Kunsthalle (until 18 April). Twenty video installations and more than 30 single-screen works include 'The Nantes Triptych', shown in Belfast last winter.

Richard Long's travels continue as a retrospective of the British sculptor's work opens at the Kunstverein in Hanover (until 14 March). This not only includes the first showing of photographs from the early 1960s, but also a new plotting technique for his wall-based text works. Watch out for large-scale new works, including a 100-metre locally quarried stone installation in the city's Orangerie. Also showing at the Kunstverein is 'Noisegate M.6' by the Austrian-based duo Granular Synthesis ("Silent Station", 13 February–14 March). *DB*

**Left: Bill Viola, 'Passage', 1987.
Above: Richard Long, 'A Line in the Himalayas', 1975**

Fast cars, fast buildings

Glasgow '99, the world's biggest festival of architecture and design, kicked off in January with a crowded programme of exhibitions and events. Organised by Deyan Sudjic, the year-long event encapsulates the breadth of design, ranging from the historic to the ultra modern, the populist to the academic, the learned to the irreverent, in a far-reaching menu that promises to provide something for everyone.

At the heart of the spring events are three major exhibitions. Sports fans everywhere will delight in the first show, "Winning: the Design of Sports" (until 5 April) at the McLellan Galleries, which examines design in sport: from Formula One racing cars to high performance materials, graphics and advertising.

At the other end of the spectrum is "Frank Lloyd Wright and the Living City" (19 February–11 April) at the Art Gallery and Museum, Kelvingrove. One of the century's best-known designers, Wright combined architecture with urban design. The exhibition illustrates both aspects of his practice – masterpieces such as the Johnson Wax administration building in Racine, Wisconsin, and urban design schemes such as Broadacre City, with models, photographs and original furniture.

Things accelerate with "Vertigo: the Strange New World of the Contemporary City" (26 February–16 March) at The Old Fruitmarket, a show which turns its attention to the vertiginous speed of change in contemporary architecture. Curated by Rowan Moore and designed by architects Caruso St John with graphic designer Peter Willberg, it takes ten of the world's most significant building projects – schemes such as the new Tate Gallery of Modern Art at Bankside, the Millennium Dome and Shanghai World Financial Centre – to show how architects are responding to the new priorities created by contemporary city building. *NS*

New priorities: the Shanghai World Financial Centre

Bushwhacked

The portrait of Victorian art critic John Ruskin (above) appears tender and affectionate. It was painted from 1853 to 1854 by John Everett Millais, whose portraiture is explored in a show at the National Portrait Gallery (19 February–6 June). Millais began the picture while on a summer trip to Scotland with Ruskin and his wife Effie. A year later he had run off with and married Effie. He learned that Ruskin had been unable to consummate the marriage on discovering, to his horror, that women had pubic hair. In a letter to Millais on receiving the painting, the apparently indifferent Ruskin wrote: "I look bored – pale – and a little too yellow." SG

Augusto Alves da Silva
Rineke Dijkstra
Alex Hartley
Yinka Shonibare
Paul M Smith

The Citibank
Private Bank
Photography Prize
1999

The Photographers' Gallery
5 & 8 Great Newport St
London WC2H 7HY
Telephone 0171 831 1772
www.photonet.org.uk
Open daily

Sponsored by

THE TIMES

6 February–
3 April

The
Photographers'
Gallery
London

Paul Smith *Make My Night*

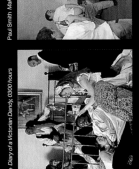
Yinka Shonibare *Diary of a Victorian Dandy, 0300 hours*

Alex Hartley *Viewer*

Rineke Dijkstra *Kolobrzeg, Poland, 26 July 1992*

Augusto Alves da Silva *Road Works*

PARIS

Heavyweight Hockney?

For those wandering the concrete expanse of Les Halles searching for cultural enlightenment the past year has been a disappointment. The temporary closure of the main wing of the Pompidou Centre has meant fewer twentieth-century masters and more advertisement hoardings accompanied by straining barrel organists. However, compensation comes in the form of the Pompidou's South Gallery, which looks set to fill the cultural void with a series of major exhibitions, together with extramural events. These are designed to widen the French public's awareness of the national collection, assisted by strategic shows across the country.

"David Hockney Espace/Paysage" (27 January-26 April) injects a hybrid of LA sun and industrial Britain into the Parisian winter mist with work from 1967 to the present day. Highlights include two vast new landscapes of the Grand Canyon devised especially for the Pompidou show. In a fine endorsement of

Bradford's boldest defector, Paris is also showing his work at La Musée Picasso in "David Hockney – Dialogue avec Picasso" (6 February-3 May) and at the Maison Européenne de la Photographie – "David Hockney – Photographies" (10 February-15 March). Although he has a significant place in post-war British art history, Hockney's adoption of a form of naturalism in the mid-1960s was felt, by some critics, to be retrogressive. These exhibitions present an opportune moment to reassess the artist, to determine whether his status as a popular figure still merits the title "lightweight".

Launching the extramural programme is "Les Années Cubistes" at the Musée d'Art Moderne Lille Metropole (13 March-15 July). Spanning the period 1907-1925, the exhibition charts the development of Analytical Cubism up to 1912 and the emergence of the equally radical and momentous Synthetic Cubism in the ensuing years. Paintings from the

Groupe de Puteaux (Marcel Duchamp, Raymond Duchamp-Villon and Jacques Villon) are exhibited alongside work by Braque and Picasso. Sculpture is represented by Alexander Archipenko, Henri Laurens and Ossip Zadkine, yet their styles are so individual it is often difficult to identify the Cubist thread that connects them.

Finally, "Mark Rothko" (8 January-18 April) at the Musée d'Art Moderne brings the highly acclaimed American show to Europe. The Tate's serene 'Seagram Murals' have travelled to Paris for the exhibition, which, together with the Pollock retrospective in London, forms a cross-Channel Ab-Ex heaven. *JL*

Above: David Hockney, 'Pearblossom Hwy, 11-18th April 1986'. Right: Luigi Ontani, 'San Sebastiano', 1998

ITALY

Early death and Secession

Bologna's newest art space – the No Code Gallery – is set to show one of Italy's emerging international figures: Luigi Ontani. A native of nearby Vergato, Ontani produces large ceramic works which are effectively stories in 3D. He has just completed a vast version of 'Cain and Abel' and continues a series begun in 1995 called 'Tribes and Taboos'. The latest additions to this ongoing ceramic comedy of errors are characters drawn from art history whose lives were cut short: from Umberto Boccioni's fatal fall while riding a horse (ironic for the man of mechanical speed), to more gruesome deaths caused by suicide, alcohol and drugs (1 April-30 May).

The Fondazione Mazzotta in Milan continues its journey through the nineteenth century with "Gustav Klimt: The Origins of Secession in Vienna" (14 February-16 May). Taken from the Graphische Sammlung Albertina collection, this important show, comprising more than 300 works, focuses on the crucial early years when Klimt turned away from the old-fashioned Künstlerhaus and set up the Viennese Secession with other artists, designers and architects. Two parallel shows are devoted to other significant, if neglected, Secessionists such as Kolo Moser and Ferdinand Andri, as well as foreign artists including Toulouse-Lautrec and Munch.

When Anselm Kiefer published his autobiography in 1976 the last entry of his book read: "The essential is not yet done." Since then his work has reinterpreted the role of the painter. Kiefer takes history, culture and national and artistic identity as his themes, employing historical references and elements of the irrational and the mystical. In a new exhibition in Rome at the Galleria Nazionale d'Arte Moderna (27 March-29 August), his canvases, which generally incorporate mixed media of photographs, lead, sand, paper and dried flowers, are now thickly painted. Does this mean the essential has arrived? *AC*

Blue interior, 1947, oil on canvas, signed, 19⅞ x 25⅛ in. 50.5 x 63.7 cm.

PETER POTWOROWSKI

1898 – 1962

Paintings and Watercolours

25 March – 30 April 1999

"...while we were all individuals before his arrival we must have seemed, thereafter, rather ordinary ...". Kenneth Armitage, 1968

"his paintings brought to us a fresh excitement and the feeling of surprise". Adrian Heath, 1958

Fully illustrated catalogue available, with foreword by Bryan Robertson

CONNAUGHT BROWN

2 ALBEMARLE STREET, LONDON W1X 3HF
TELEPHONE 0171-408 0362. FAX 0171- 495 3137
http://www.connaught-brown.co.uk

POLISH AIRLINES
Sponsored by

Patrick Caulfield

Interior landscape

"I hate orange. Well, I dislike orange. But I use it, perversely, because I dislike it. I force myself to use it." Patrick Caulfield has forced himself to use the colour orange throughout an influential career spanning four decades. It is a strange paradox – but paradox is Caulfield's art. Walk round his retrospective at the Hayward Gallery (4 February-11 April) and you'll sense an unnerving familiarity as well as recognise his love/hate relationship with gaudy colours.

Caulfield is our most seductive painter of the urban. He has made it OK to paint the grubby world of cafés, bars and dull domestic interiors. The sad, sagging reality of textured Vymura paint, the garish plastic flowers, naff Greek restaurants with polypropylene chairs all form a vocabulary that is so close to home that we don't know whether to smirk or cringe. These spaces may not exist in real life but we've all been there. "Social realism without the emotion," is how Caulfield describes it.

Caulfield's world is not a simple side-swipe at decorative art or neo-Pop filled with throwaway gesture. This is an English art that fuses an almost Orwellian focus on the ordinariness of our daily surroundings with an intangible celebration through colour and form. It is fun and depressing; psychology over documentary.

His preoccupation with interiors and still lifes places him in a British tradition that links him to Sickert and Gilman rather than the Pop generation (Hockney and Jones) with whom Caulfield emerged from the Royal College of Art in 1960. Sickert's ability to paraphrase private ennui opened up a new world of painterly possibilities. It was later taken up in the 1950s by Kitchen Sink painters such as John Bratby, whom Caulfield admires. They share an unashamed embrace of gloomy subjects and its fly-on-the-wall look at life in the slow lane. However, Caulfield is the better anthropologist. He says far more about the confused twentieth century and its amalgam of influences than Bratby. Bratby was tied to his sink, Caulfield uses it as a prop.

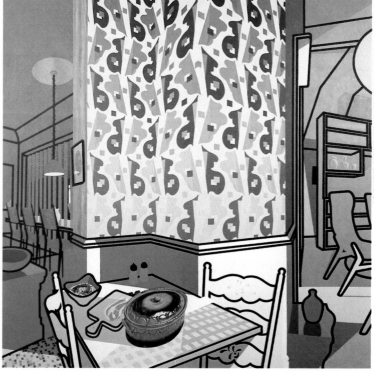

But he does not spoon-feed his anthropology. It emerges through his subtle visual humour, through images that quietly tease the viewer, both in content and in composition.

The mixture of imagery – a painted piece of meat, a photograph of an alpine landscape, the abstract blocks of colour – blends together in a way that plays with reality. Sometimes it feels more real than the paint. "The reason I do some part of the painting real," says Caulfield, "is to make the other things real by interpretation."

Somewhere in here we can find echoes of Léger's colourful simplicity, Gris's playful perspectives and Magritte's wit. His work has all the trappings of Pop – the ironic detachment and the non-fine art sources – but has none of Pop's narrative or its interest in large scale. It is a displacement with which we can sympathise, an "other world" which, despite its retro hints, never seems to date. As with Edward Hopper's paintings, time is distorted, slowed down, producing a sense of melancholy through absence. We can feel a longing, but this is soon checked by the fiction of the situation.

What keeps us moving through Caulfield's work is its lack of sentimentality. A loving touch is at work here, one that has faith in the complexities of the modern world. Perhaps he has become our great landscape painter; the landscape painter of the interior. It is these spaces, after all, in which we spend much of our lives – working and living, laughing and crying, or just staring into space. *SG*

Patrick Caulfield, 'Dining/Kitchen/Living', 1980, (above); 'Registry Office', 1997, (far left); 'Inside a Swiss Chalet', 1969, (left)

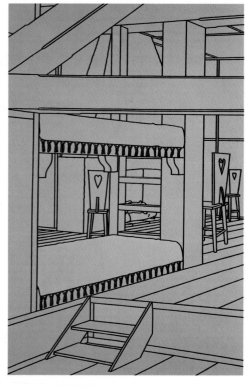

Marlborough

Polly and Duck 1996-98, oil on canvas, 85½ x 54½ in.

CHRISTOPHER BRAMHAM

27 January – 27 February 1999

Marlborough Fine Art (London) Ltd

6 Albemarle Street London W1X 4BY
Telephone (0171) 629 5161 Telefax (0171) 495 0641

Courtesy Norman Foster and Partners

Ar(t)chitectural alliance

Few parliament buildings can boast as prominent a place in the contemporary art world as the Berlin Reichstag. First Christo wrapped its exterior, turning the florid *fin-de-siècle* building into a giant installation piece. Now, British architect Sir Norman Foster has reworked the interior and roof giving it a whole new life and a crisply contemporary addition.

Abandoned 50 years ago when Germany's great post-war statesman Konrad Adenauer moved his parliament to Bonn, the Reichstag building reopens this spring when Berlin resumes its position as the country's seat of government. But when Bundestag members arrive for the first session they will find a very different building from the one they turned their back on half a century ago.

Foster's designs may reveal the building's history – original stonework (some of it shell-marked), charred timbers and graffiti from the Russian occupation are all visible – but its emphasis is more firmly on the contemporary. It is the world's first public building to be powered by renewable energy – in this case

vegetable oil from sunflower seeds and rape.

Back in the UK, Foster's is one of the practices working on the long-awaited Jubilee Line extension. His station at Canary Wharf is not scheduled to open until later in the year but this spring should see the first tranche of stations coming on line. With each one designed by a different architect, the ride provides a journey through the best of contemporary British architecture, from Alsop & Störmer's flamboyant exoticism at North Greenwich, through Troughton McAslan's sleek minimalism at Canning Town, via Van Heyningen &

Haward's soft modernism at West Ham and ending with Chris Wilkinson's high-tech at Stratford.

Not that you have to live in the south to experience the best of British design. Far from it. Residents of Sheffield will have noticed the National Centre for Popular Music going up in the city's expanding cultural quarter. The building, which opens this March, is described by its architects Branson Coates as "a juke box allowing for randomly accessible events". Interactive exhibition space is housed in four vast stainless steel drums, themselves reminders of Sheffield's industrial history. *NS*

© Branson Coates Architecture/Nigel Coates

Above: the new German Reichstag building, Berlin. Right: the National Centre for Popular Music, Sheffield

Art in a flash

Late summer is usually a quiet time in the Australian art calendar, but that's not a reason to avoid the galleries. They're cool, airy… and empty. And if you want to escape the blistering heat, there's plenty to see.

The National Gallery of Australia in Canberra is hosting three diverse shows. "In a Flash" (until 15 March) celebrates the ground-breaking work of Harold E Edgerton, who introduced the stroboscope to photography, making it possible to create instantaneous pictures of fast moving objects. During the 1930s and 1940s, Edgerton experimented with various subjects, from drops of milk to bullets (as in 'Playing Card', 1964). The motivation was science, the results – spectacular art.

Emily Kame Kngwarreye was in her eighties before she was discovered. The NGA's retrospective of her vibrant paintings reveals her distinctive vision of the land, both recognisably Aboriginal and highly original (13 February-18 April). Not surprisingly, her work has spawned a generation of imitators.

Forming a different kind of line, "Matisse: the Art of Drawing" (20 March-11 July) showcases 100 drawings, prints and books, dating from 1906 to 1947 and either owned by the NGA or loaned by other Australian institutions. Unlike Kngwarreye, whose compositions were more subconscious, Matisse focused on visual immediacy: a master draughtsman of the old school.

If it's February in Sydney, it must be Mardi Gras. "Look!" is the annual gay festival's visual arts extravaganza. This year's event is happening in 21 galleries, though "galleries" should be taken loosely. "All That Glitters", by Andy Davey, is a truck that cruises the streets for twelve hours a day bearing a huge gilded ad to test the presumptive qualities of gold (20-27 February).

Elsewhere in Sydney, you can catch the final weeks of "Classic Cézanne" at the Art Gallery of New South Wales (until 28 February). Remarkably, it is Cézanne's first solo show in this country. It features 82 works from more than 30 museums around the world and is wide-ranging, with watercolours and drawings as well as 30 of his best paintings. *RdeL*

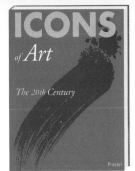
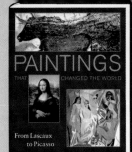
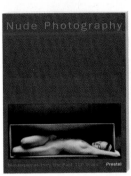

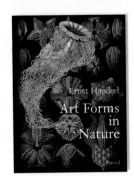

PORTUGAL

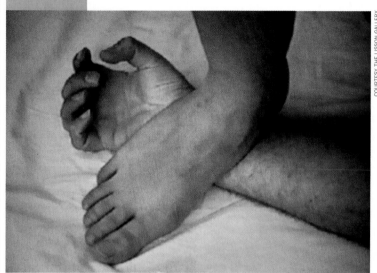

Laying cultural foundations

Portugal has been quietly edging its way on to the contemporary art map. Between 1994, when Lisbon was European Cultural Capital, and 1998, when the same city hosted Expo 98, several art institutions have pushed forward their international focus. Likewise in Oporto, Lisbon's rival, new developments are ensuring the country's continued cultural expansion.

The Serralves Foundation is the key venue in Oporto, presiding over the opening of a clutch of new commercial galleries. Under the directorship of Vicente Todoli, previously of Valencia's IVAM and an assistant curator to Giovanni Carrandente at the last Venice Biennale, the Foundation opens its eagerly awaited Museum of Contemporary Art within its own gardens in June. Designed by the acclaimed Portuguese architect Álvaro Siza, it will include multiple exhibition spaces as well as an auditorium and documentation centre. The museum will house the Foundation's collection dating from the mid-1960s, as well as staging major contemporary shows. The retrospective of young Scottish artist Christine Borland (10 April–23 May) is the last exhibition to take place in the Foundation Museum before the new building opens.

Meanwhile in Lisbon, the Centro Cultural de Belém (a huge cultural complex overlooking the River Tagus in one of the more spacious, beautiful areas of Lisbon) heralded the new year with two significant exhibitions, by Douglas Gordon (recipient of the $50,000 Hugo Boss prize) and João Penalva (until 9 May).

Gordon's exhibition includes several trademark pieces, not least '24 Hour Psycho', 'Hysterical' and 'Thirty Second Text', as well as three conceived for the venue. 'What You Want Me to Say' is a sound and text work based on a scene from John Boulting's 1947 film classic, *Brighton Rock*: the constantly repeated recording of Gordon's own voice issuing from twelve loudspeakers, saying "I love you" and followed by the click of a broken record, evokes a sense of longing filled with both cruelty and paradox.

Penalva, born in Portugal and long resident in England, has also been establishing a higher profile over the past few years. He shows six works dating from the 1990s, including 'Wallenda', a record (both audio and visual) of an undertaking as absurd as it is epic – to whistle Stravinsky's entire *Rite of Spring*.

Drawing upon his experience as a dancer and then a painter, Penalva's

Left: Douglas Gordon, 'Hand and Foot, (right)', 1996. Top: the Museum of Contemporary Art, Oporto. Above: Christine Borland, 'From Life', 1994

recent work combines an elaborate process of research with a performative dexterity and formal precision. He uses diverse means (sound, video, collections of readymade objects and archival material) to stage works underwritten by elusive and teasing narratives which move between fact and fiction, identity and authorship: "I want to be as many minds as I can". *RR*

Weird science

The Piers Arts Centre in Stromness on Orkney is staging 'The Way Stations' (right), a work by Matthew Dalziel and Louise Scullion (27 March–8 May).

The piece consists of a series of images, ambiguous in both scale and meaning, in which anonymous constructions resembling silos or faceless scientific institutes sit in bleak landscapes. It echoes the duo's previous projects where photography, sound and video were installed directly in the landscape, a literal juxtaposition of technology and nature. Here, science is depicted as a new religion, its buildings like monasteries or retreats; but is it a threat or an opportunity for salvation? *RW*

Stony weather

Inspired by the wind-swept coastline of St Ives, 'Quoit Monserrat', 1998, (below) is a new work by the Barbara Hepworth Museum's artist-in-residence, Veronica Ryan. Sculpted from a large slab of uncut marble found in Hepworth's studio, it forms part of the "Artists' Projects" programme at the Tate Gallery St Ives (until 11 April). *JL*

New books from Thames and Hudson

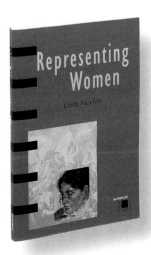

Representing Women
LINDA NOCHLIN
A partly autobiographical introduction
introduces this important collection of
writings by the renowned art historian.
With 170 illustrations
Paperback £14.95 March

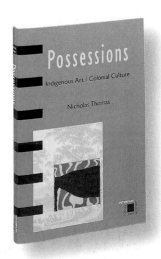

Possessions
Indigenous Art/Colonial Culture
NICHOLAS THOMAS
This revelatory book explores the complex
relationship between tribal art and modern
Western art.
With 183 illustrations, 20 in colour
Paperback £16.95 March

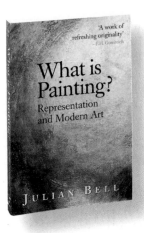

What is Painting?
Representation and Modern Art
JULIAN BELL
'So vivid in its thinking and so propelled in its
narration that I find it difficult to be other than
astonished and admiring' – John Elderfield
With 158 illustrations, 16 in colour
Paperback £12.95 April

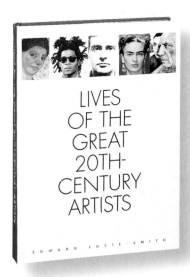

Lives of the Great 20th-Century Artists
EDWARD LUCIE-SMITH
One hundred pioneers of modern art, from
Picasso to Louise Bourgeois and Jean-Michel
Basquiat, are presented here in well-illustrated
and revealing biographies.
With 273 illustrations, 101 in colour £24.95 May

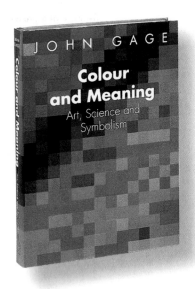

Colour and Meaning
Art, Science and Symbolism
JOHN GAGE
John Gage, Reader in the History of Western
Art, University of Cambridge, expands his
discussion of the topics and issues hinted at in his
previous prize-winning book *Colour and Culture*.
With 137 illustrations, 37 in colour £32.00 April

Egon Schiele
The Complete Works
JANE KALLIR
WITH AN ESSAY BY WOLFGANG G. FISCHER
Expanded edition, with a biography,
and catalogue raisonné including 205
new entries.
*With over 3,275 illustrations, including 94 plates
in full colour and 107 in duotone £95.00*

For details of our new and forthcoming publications, please write to Promotions Department, **Thames and Hudson** 181A High Holborn, London WC1V 7QX

The ambiguous precision of Francis Bacon

In a posthumous scandal which Bacon would have relished, the role of drawing in his art is now being reassessed. Rory Snookes examines the painter's reputation for spontaneity

In 1962, in the catalogue essay accompanying Bacon's first Tate retrospective, the then director of the gallery, Sir John Rothenstein, contrasted the "precisely formulated intention" embodied by the Tate's 'Three Studies for Figures at the Base of a Crucifixion' (c.1944) with the "blind inspiration" which he believed had given rise to the MoMA work, 'Painting 1946'. His assessment of Bacon's achievement, whom he characterised as "a sort of figurative action-painter working under the spell of the subconscious", evidently met with the artist's approval, its basic premise being reiterated by him (most effectively in conversation with the art critic David Sylvester) until his death in 1992.

For 30 years, Bacon's prodigious theorising served to obscure important aspects of his working method – aspects, it transpires, more associated with "precisely formulated intentions" than with "blind inspiration". For though, in later life, Bacon was inclined towards demystifying his approach to painting, he remained unwilling (publicly at least) to discuss, even to acknowledge, his propensity for drawing and sketching.

Monkey business?

Last year, having examined material originating from a number of different sources, curators at the Tate acquired a book entitled *Introducing Monkeys*. It contained hand-written lists of potential subjects for paintings, a number of reproductions of works the artist is thought to have destroyed and 40 interleaved works on paper, all of which had belonged to Bacon's friends Paul Danquah and Peter Pollock, with whom he shared

accommodation between 1955 and 1961. Four additional oil sketches were bought from relatives of the late Stephen Spender, to whom they had been given during the early 1960s, yet which had not come to public notice until their inclusion in Bacon's Pompidou/Haus der Kunst retrospective in 1996-1997. The majority of these works have been reliably dated, stylistically and through their provenance (in an extensive catalogue essay), to c.1957-1961, a period during which Bacon's art suffered radical change, culminating in the development of his mature style.

This spring (until 2 May) a selection of these (mostly) previously unpublished works is on show alongside early and contemporaneous examples of Bacon's "public" paintings from the Tate's collection.

The discovery of a substantial body of such work during the past few years, all of it post-dating the 'Three Studies for Figures at the Base of a Crucifixion', has cast into doubt Bacon's claims regarding the spontaneity of his mature style and has caused indignation in some quarters, leading to his being posthumously accused of "cruelly and deliberately making fools of friends and admirers" (Edward Lucie-Smith, "Bacon's Unseen Sketches", *Art Review*, December/January 1999). The preparatory status of the offending works, however, is open to question, for though some of them clearly relate to paintings from Bacon's established *oeuvre*, the nature of their relationship is unclear. Bacon habitually and openly referred to reproductions of his own works while painting and produced "second versions" of both 'Painting 1946', in

1971, and 'Three Studies for Figures at the Base of a Crucifixion', in 1988. It seems admissible to interpret those sketches most closely resembling already familiar paintings as copies made after the completion of the larger works, rather than as studies made beforehand.

Bacon's proclaimed abstinence from drawing is clearly a distortion of the truth, but his remarks regarding its ultimate practical limitations are borne out by the evidence of the paintings themselves. During the course of the last of his interviews with David Sylvester, Bacon casually mentioned his tendency, when beginning a painting, to "sketch out very roughly on the canvas with a brush, just a vague outline of something" (*Interview 9*, 1984-1986). The "accidental" element of his paintings, from the late 1940s onwards, is to be found not so much in their compositional whole, but in the structure of their figuration. While the placement and, to an extent, the posture of his figures might be derived from preparatory sources, the peculiarities of their internal modelling, particularly the structure of their heads and their facial expression, can be seen to have resulted from exactly the kind of sabotaged illustration frequently cited by the artist as forming the basis of his painterly vocabulary.

In the mid-1950s Bacon had begun to explore the possibility of further reducing the "illustrational" (literal) content of his already spare descriptive means. 'Two Figures in the Grass', painted in 1954, features thoroughly abstract passages

TATE GALLERY

'Figure in a Landscape', c.1952. Facing page: Bacon's reworked images of the boxers Georges Carpentier (left) and Jack Dempsey, c.1957-1961

incorporated into an unprecedentedly loose, but highly suggestive, figurative framework. This was also evident in a sketch from 1952 called 'Figure in a Landscape'. The expressionistic brushwork and dramatically brightened palette of the 'Study for Portrait of van Gogh' series, painted in 1957, seem to express Bacon's frustration at having run up against the formal barrier of figurative legibility. In most of these paintings the figure of van Gogh, taken from the latter's 'The Painter on the Road to Tarascon' (1888, destroyed), is reduced to an irregular silhouette, their only remaining illustrational detail being that used to describe the artist's hat. By 1962, Bacon had begun to speak of wanting to make his figuration "more and more precise; but of a very ambiguous precision" (David Sylvester, *Interview 1*, 1962).

Transparent figuration

One of the most elaborate of the Tate's new works, 'Figure in a Grey Interior', features a distinctive curved aperture, first used in 'Study for Crouching Nude' (1952), then again in the Tate's 'Study for Portrait on Folding Bed' (1963), upon which has been placed a crouching or kneeling figure. The composition seems to have been initially established in casual, but relatively literal, pencil outline, then given substance through rapid and extensive brushwork, pink and blue oil paint being used respectively to help to distinguish the subject from its surroundings. In this, and other oil sketches, drawn and painted figurative elements remain disunited, the latter appearing to float above the former, weakening instead of strengthening their structural relationship, resulting in a form of figuration characterised by its relative opacity or transparency, rather than by its three-dimensionality.

Most of the works on paper have been rendered using a brush too large in relation to the overall size of the image to allow for much intricacy of detail. However, a small number of unpainted works, some drawn in graphite, others in biro, seem concerned with quite specific formal problems and it is these drawings which demonstrate most eloquently the nature and the limit of the contribution made by the works on paper to those on canvas. One drawing in particular, 'Seated Woman', clearly exhibits the postural

CARPENTIER—BOGEYMAN
TO

JOE BECKETT v. GEORGES CARPENTIER

Joe Beckett, British heavy-weight champion, was twice a one-round victim to Georges Carpentier, a great light-heavy-weight, who caused havoc among the heavy-weights of Europe. Their first fight (above) took place at Holborn Stadium, London, on December 4, 1919, the second at Olympia, London, on October 1, 1923—both with the same result. One or two sporting writers started up a controversy in which it was alleged François Descamps, Carpentier's manager, put an hypnotic eye on Beckett. All that really happened was that Georges each time put an hypnotic right on Joe's chin.

25

JACK DEMPSEY

Born Manassa, Colorado, June 24, 1895. Nationality, Irish-Scottish-American. Began boxing in 1914 as Kid Blackie. His partnership with Jack "Doc" Kearns became one of the ring's greatest romances. After battering Willard, he figured in five million-dollar gates. Although beaten for the title by Tunney in 1926, the name of Dempsey still carries magic.

revisions and distortions associated with Bacon's "non-illustrational" oil paintings. Its subject's left foot, pointed outwards at first, away from its body, has been reversed, its toes planted against the floor, its heel raised; its head, initially faced forwards, has, moments later, been pushed to one side, into profile, beneath heavier, darker revisionary drawing. Work of this nature could well have served a more conventional preparatory purpose than the broadly painted oil sketches, its linearity bearing formal information more readily translatable from small scale into large.

Bacon's first recorded disavowal of preparatory work, made just after the period from which the Tate's works on paper are thought to date, was couched in terms intended to emphasise the spontaneity of his working method: "As the actual texture, colour, the whole way the paint moves are so accidental," he said in 1962, "any sketches that I did before could only give a kind of

skeleton, possibly, of the way the thing might happen."

His use of the word "skeleton" in this context is suggestive of a rigidly graphic, internal framework. In fact, the majority of Bacon's oil sketches serve more in the capacity of an exoskeleton than an endoskeleton, providing the model for an irregular boundary within which the fluid brushwork of the larger paintings might be contained.

Drawing conclusions

Nowhere is this figurative approach more evident than in two overpainted pages, once belonging to an illustrated history of boxing, bought along with the Danquah/Pollock cache of sketches, in which the athletic stance of the figures of Georges Carpentier and Jack Dempsey has been transformed, through the bold application of black oil paint, into postures immediately suggestive of the kind of convulsive figuration inhabiting Bacon's large-scale works. The image of the boxer Jack

Dempsey has been partially obscured beneath an invasive, brightly coloured background in a manner duplicated by most of the familiar paintings of this period.

Bacon's insistent dismissal of illustrational formal language is inextricably linked to the impression made upon him, from an early age, by photography and film and, more precisely, by the capacity of both media to record the passage of time. As early as 1949, he had begun to consult and appropriate Eadweard Muybridge's late nineteenth-century photographic sequences recording human and animal motion. David Sylvester, writing in 1952, noted the "casual, transitory positions" adopted by Bacon's figures, making them seem "caught unawares in a candid camera shot". From the outset of his career, Bacon chose to assert his modernity through referencing diverse photographic material, ostensibly in place of sketches and drawings. The Tate's works on paper can be seen to provide invaluable

insight into the role of photography in the development of Bacon's mature style. A remark made by the artist to Sir John Rothenstein suggests a link between the incidental formal effects associated with photography and those commonly resulting from the process of sketching rapidly in miniature. Indicating a photograph of a panicked crowd, taken in St Petersburg during the revolution, Bacon drew attention to the massive distortions suffered by the tiny images of people "caught in violent motion", describing one figure in particular as being "utterly unlike the conventional concept of a man running". It seems likely that painting or drawing swiftly, on a small scale, with a relatively large brush (often working after photographic sources) provided Bacon with a ready means of generating exaggerated formal irregularities analogous to those observed by him in photography.
"Francis Bacon: Works on Paper and Paintings", Tate Gallery, London, 24 February–2 May

PETER PRENDERGAST

New Paintings 1994-98

20 March - 8 May

48pp catalogue, 24 colour plates, essay by John Russell Taylor
£7.95 inc. p&p ISBN 0 906860 41 5

Oriel Mostyn Art Gallery
T: +44 (0)1492 879201 F: +44 (0)1492 878869 E: art@orielmostyn.demon.co.uk

An Oriel Mostyn Art Gallery touring exhibtion

Bethan Huws

Watercolours

15 May - 3 July

180pp catalogue, 60 colour plates, essays by Julian Heynen, Ulrich Loock and
Josef Helfenstein £17.50 inc. p&p ISBN 3 926530 83 9

Oriel Mostyn Art Gallery
12 Vaughan Street, Llandudno, LL30 1AB, UK

An Oriel Mostyn Art Gallery exhibtion in collaboration with
Kaiser Wilhelm Museum, Krefeld, and Kuntsmeuseum, Bern

---

martin boyce
january / march

stephan jung
march / april

jonathan hammer
april / may

t. +44 (0)171 636 2221
f. +44 (0)171 436 6067
e. clever@easynet.co.uk
51 CLEVELAND ST LONDON WIP 5PQ

gallery artists

liz arnold

cindy bernard

roderick buchanan

monica carocci

jason coburn

cheryl donegan

moyna flannigan

david griffiths

graham gussin

pierre huyghe

tracy mackenna & edwin janssen

mariele neudecker

VICTORIA MIRO GALLERY

3 March – 9 April 1999

CONTEMPLATING POLLOCK

Thomas Demand
Peter Doig
Andreas Gursky

Marina Abramovic
Cecily Brown
Thomas Demand
Peter Doig
Ian Hamilton Finlay
Andreas Gursky
Alex Hartley
Chantal Joffe
Isaac Julien
Udomsak Krisanamis
Yayoi Kusama
Abigail Lane
Brad Lochore
Robin Lowe
Nicholas May
Dawn Mellor
Tracey Moffatt
Chris Ofili
Gary Perkins
Hadrian Pigott
Inez Van Lamsweerde
Stephen Willats

21 Cork Street London W1X 1HB Tel: 0171 734 5082 Fax: 0171 494 1787

Thomas Demand "Scheune" (Barn) 1997, chromogenic print on photographic paper and Diasec 183.5 x 254 cm

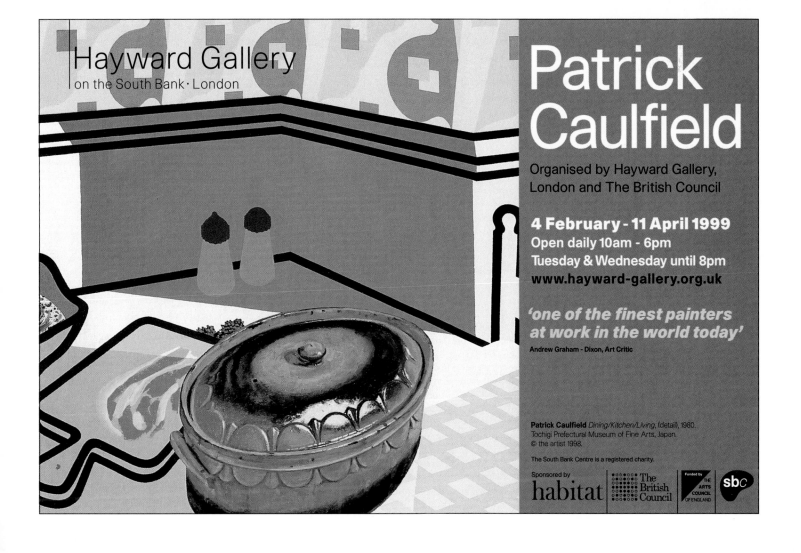

Hayward Gallery
on the South Bank · London

Patrick
Caulfield

Organised by Hayward Gallery,
London and The British Council

4 February - 11 April 1999
Open daily 10am - 6pm
Tuesday & Wednesday until 8pm
www.hayward-gallery.org.uk

'one of the finest painters
at work in the world today'
Andrew Graham - Dixon, Art Critic

Patrick Caulfield *Dining/Kitchen/Living*, (detail), 1980.
Tochigi Prefectural Museum of Fine Arts, Japan.
© the artist 1998.

The South Bank Centre is a registered charity.

Sponsored by
habitat   The British Council   THE ARTS COUNCIL OF ENGLAND   sbc

Framed
Henri Michaux

'The Mescaline Series' was produced as an hallucinogenic experiment during the 1950s. Simon Grant surveys the work of the reluctant junkie

When Henri Michaux (1899-1984) was a little boy he wouldn't eat his food. He spurned family life, preferring an isolated existence, buried in books and dreaming about seeing exotic countries. He fulfilled his dreams as an adult, travelling to South America, Turkey and Asia over ten years. It was an important formative period for him, laying the foundations for his more meditative explorations.

Often placed within the Paris post-war aesthetic, Michaux, the Belgian/French poet and painter, was regarded as a "key witness to the existential crisis of the twentieth century", a man burdened with personal suffering (his first wife, Marie-Louise, died in 1948). True enough, his early writings reflect the image of an anguished man battling with a sense of purpose (as explored in his book *My Properties* of 1929). And his half abstract, half figurative works fitted neatly into the existential turmoil associated with Wols, Giacometti and other contemporaries. However, Michaux was not a tortured soul. He was a curious man with a clinical mind who wanted answers. And he looked to the powerful hallucinogenic drug, mescaline, to find them.

Under the supervision of a prominent Spanish neurologist, Julian

de Ajuriaguerra, he began in 1954, along with a number of other "subjects", to ingest the drug and then write down his experiences. He also made remarkable drawings, now collectively known as the 'Mescaline Series'. They are feverish, intense scribblings that follow a clear, almost cinematic continuity and work extraordinarily well in tandem with his writings on the subject. However, it was not an easy task for him. Michaux loathed his trips. He was a reluctant junkie and his journals are littered with nightmarish visions and endless sessions of torture:

Must I talk about pleasure? It was unpleasant.

Thus, and always at that relentless, inhuman speed, I was assaulted, pierced by the electric mole burrowing its way through the most personal essence of my person.

Trapped, not in something human, but in a frantic mechanical shaker, in a mixer-crusher-crumbler, treated like metal in a factory, like water in a turbine, like wind in a wind tunnel, like roots in an automatic wood-grinder, like iron in the tireless motion of steel lathes turning out gears. But I had to remain conscious.

The main horror of it was that I was only a line. In normal life, you're a sphere, a sphere that comes upon panoramas. Here only a line. A line breaking into a thousand aberrations.

It's so absolutely horrible, horrible in its essence. I can't find any way of saying it and I feel like a counterfeiter when I try. My perturbation was great. The devastation was greater.

Michaux's writings of his experiences were to become of great interest to the medical profession, for here was a drug taker explaining the neurological effects. He had trained as a doctor (although he never completed the course), so took on the role of the intellectual observer. Aldous Huxley, writing in *The Doors of Perception*, had attempted a similar goal of explaining the effects of hallucinogens, but for a more literary end. Michaux published three seminal works on the subject: *Miserable Miracle* (1956), *Turbulent Infinity* (1957) and *Knowledge Through the Abyss* (1961). The titles sum up his relationship with drug taking. His insatiable curiosity demanded that he

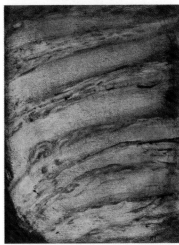

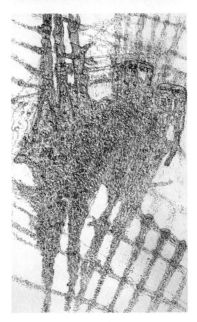

find some kind of truth, but at great expense, and throughout the three books we hear him weighing up the cost of his mental state with the results he hopes to achieve:

In great discomfort, in anguish, in inner solemnity. The world pulling away to some distance, a growing distance. Each word becoming dense, too dense to be pronounced from now on… while the sound of wood cracking in the fireplace becomes the only presence, becomes important: preoccupying and strange in its movements… Waiting, a wait that gets heavier every minute, that listens more, grows indescribable, more painful to carry with me… and how far can I carry it?

No matter how confined he may have been, the Machiavellian feat resulted in some remarkable drawings. The excessive stimulation produced for him dazzling, loud, shocking colours; brutal and vulgar. The drawings echo Michaux's obsession with the speed of thoughts and visions that ran through his mind. Rivers, furrows and tree-like shapes appear repeatedly:

So it came, pouring forth. But more violently, more electrically, more fantastically.

With my eyes closed, I watched in a vision a sort of vertical torrent come tumbling down. The long vibratile carpet which had something in common with a discharge of electricity, sparks branching out… burning, seething, like spasms for nerves, this tree with delicate branches… ready to bubble forth but held back elastically and prevented from overflowing by some kind of surface tension, this nervous projection screen, even more mysterious than visions which alighted there, I do not know, nor will I ever know, how to speak fittingly of it.

The act of drawing his experiences was important for Michaux, but it opened him up to fresh challenges: "It is not in the mirror that one should contemplate oneself," he wrote, "men, look at yourselves in the paper." The effect of a blank piece of paper under the influence of mescaline was perhaps the hardest challenge:

And 'White' appears. Absolute white. White beyond all whiteness. White of the coming of the White. White

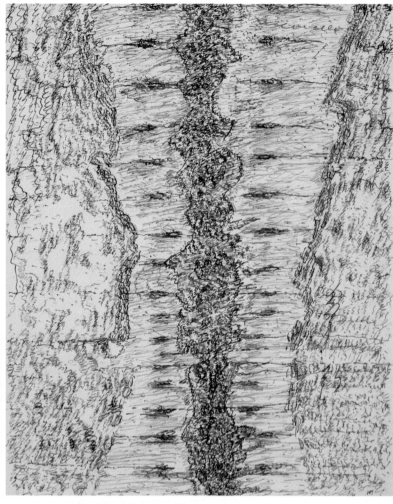

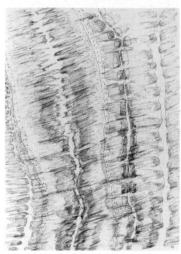

without compromise, through exclusion, through total eradication of non-white. Insane, enraged white, screaming with whiteness. Fanatical, furious, riddling the retina. Horrible electric white, implacable, murderous. White in bursts of white. God of 'white'. No, not a god, a howler monkey. (Let's hope my cells don't blow apart.) End of white. I have a feeling that for a long time to come white is going to have something excessive for me.

He was right. His experiences of mescaline were to give him ophthalmic migraines for the rest of his life. Often the challenge of white space would affect his drawing style, according to his surviving wife Micheline Phankim: "In order to fill a page he would spend hours drawing."

Michaux is honest about the limitations and pitfalls that his drug taking creates. He acknowledges that his relationship – as the observer and cataloguer – is a difficult one:

You start writing long strips of meaningless superlatives… there are also bursts of uncontrollable laughter, equally meaningless… Don't forget you've swallowed a toxic substance. Psychological explanations – too tempting. To see psychology everywhere is to lack psychology.

To enjoy a drug, you have to like being a subject.

I was distracted and tired of being distracted looking through a microscope. What's supernatural about it? One doesn't really get away from one's humanity. One felt more like a prisoner in a mental workshop.

Michaux gave up his experiments with mescaline and repeatedly issued disclaimers about his alleged addiction, but he was still writing about its effects as late as 1971.

Despite the clinical content of his observations, which appealed to specialists in psychosomatic disorders and other psychiatric lines of inquiry, at the heart of Michaux's quest lay a sympathy with the more mystical and inexplicable aspects of his research. His eloquent observations make for good reading. His 'Mescaline Series' drawings have a similar immediacy and give us an illuminating insight into an intense and curious mind. His inquiry was academic, while the exploits of, say, Timothy Leary or Hunter S

Thompson are more concerned with the literary by-products that drugs help to formulate. Perhaps if Michaux were around today, we might find him in a nightclub, standing alone, gnashing on ecstasy, watching a mass of bodies dancing and trying to work it all out. Perhaps he would have reached the same conclusions, drawn the same drawings, got the same headaches.

"After years of not taking any hallucinatory drugs," he wrote in *Emergences – Resurgences* in 1972, "the tendency to break up into fragments remains. I sometimes see the drawings I compose, decompose and divide without end…."
"Henri Michaux", Whitechapel Art Gallery, 19 February-25 April

Facing page. Claude Cahun, double portrait of Henri Michaux. From top: 'Mescaline Drawing', c.1956-1958; 'First Mescaline Drawing', c.1954; 'Post Mescaline Drawing', c.1962. Above left: 'Mescaline Drawing', c.1956-1958. Left: 'Post Mescaline Drawing', c.1966-1969. Top: 'Post Mescaline Drawing', c.1969. Above: 'Mescaline Drawing', c.1956

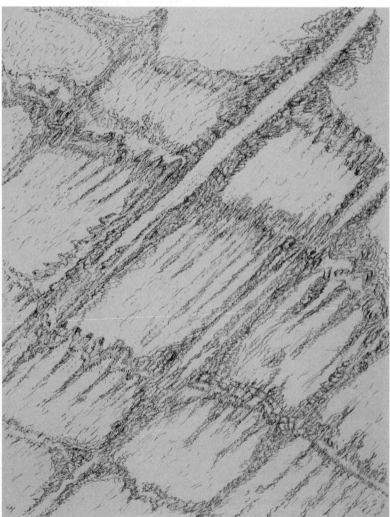

Tate Gallery Exhibitions and Events

TATE GALLERY LONDON
EXHIBITIONS

Jackson Pollock
11 March-6 June
In association with American Airlines

Chris Burden
2 March-13 June
Sponsored by American Airlines

Art Now
Programme supported by the Patrons
of New Art and Hereford Salon

Thomas Demand
16 February-25 April

Doris Salcedo
11 May-18 July

Turner's Later Papers, 1820-51
16 March-13 June

Turner in the Alps
Until 14 February
Sponsored by Lombard Odier & Cie

**In Celebration: The Art of the
Country House**
Until 28 February
Sponsored by Aon Risk Services Ltd.
In association with ITT
London & Edinburgh

New Displays
Sponsored by British Petroleum
since 1990

EVENTS
The Tate offers a full programme of
talks, conferences and films. For
details and tickets see *Tate Events*
leaflet or telephone 0171 887 8604

Chris Burden
Wednesday 3 March 18.30
The renowned American artist talks
about his work. £7 (£3.50 concs)

**Francis Bacon: Not in His Own
Words**
Sunday 28 February 13.30
Half-day conference reconsiders
Bacon following the discovery of
works on paper by the man who
denied the use of drawing in his art.
£15 (£10 concs)

The Joseph Beuys Lecture 1999
What is Good Painting – Who Knows?
Friday 12 March 18.30
An exploration of modern and recent
painting by Dore Ashton and Stephen
Farthing. In collaboration with the
Laboratory at the Ruskin School of
Drawing and Fine Art, Oxford
University. £7 (£3.50 concs)

JG Ballard
Wednesday 24 March 18.30
JG Ballard discusses images that have
made an impact on his life with art
critic William Feaver. In collaboration
with Feaver and Digney Productions
and *The Art Newspaper*.
£7 (£3.50 concs)

Kurt Pantzer Memorial Lecture
Thursday 22 April 18.30
David Blayney Brown talks on
Turner's 'War and Peace'. Tickets are
free but booking is necessary.
Sponsored by the Turner Society

TATE GALLERY LIVERPOOL
EXHIBITIONS

**Richard Deacon: New
World Order**
20 February-16 May
Supported by the Henry Moore
Foundation

Modern British Art
Until 2000

Violent Incident
27 March-March 2000

Victor Pasmore
1 May-March 2000

EVENTS
Tate Gallery Liverpool runs a full
programme of events. For details
please telephone 0151 709 3223

**International symposium on
Richard Deacon**
Saturday 24 April
A major international symposium
exploring Richard Deacon's work

TATE GALLERY ST IVES
EXHIBITIONS

**Displays 1998-9:
Partnerships and Practice**
Until 11 April

**English Roots: Artist's
Project by Eric Cameron**
Until 11 April

**Quoit Montserrat: Artist's
Project by Veronica Ryan**
Until 11 April

**As Dark as Light: New Work in
Response to the Solar Eclipse**
21 May-31 October

EVENTS
The Tate Gallery St Ives runs a full
programme of events and activities.
For further information please call
01736 796226. There are guided tours
Tuesday – Saturday at 14.30. Tours
are free with gallery admission

Poetry Reading by Sue Hubbard
Tues 23 February 19.30. £3.50/£2.50
Sue Hubbard reads from her
Everything Begins with the Skin

Inhabiting Space
Thurs 11 March 19.30. £3.50/£2.50
A lecture by artist in residence
Lubaina Himid and Dr Penny
Florence, director of research at
Falmouth College of Art

Artists' Talks
*Thursday 8 & 15 April and Saturday
10 & 17 April 14.00. Free*
Veronica Ryan talks about her work
currently on display at Tate St Ives

**Modernism and the St Ives
Writings of Virginia Woolf**
Saturday 17 April 10.00-16.00
A day school in conjunction with the
University of Exeter, based at Talland
House and Tate St Ives. For details
please call 01872 274503

**The Tate Gallery
wishes to thank its
Spring 1999 Sponsors**

Principal Corporate Sponsors
The British Petroleum Company plc
Tate & Lyle PLC

Corporate Sponsors
American Airlines
Aon Risk Services Ltd
In association with ITT London & Edinburgh
The Hiscox Group
Morgan Stanley Dean Witter
Tarmac Group plc

**Corporate
Members**

Partner Level
The British Petroleum Company plc
Ernst & Young
Freshfields
Merrill Lynch Mercury
Prudential
Unilever

Associate Level
Alliance & Leicester plc
American Express
BUPA
Channel Four Television
Compaq
Credit Suisse First Boston
De La Rue plc
Drivers Jonas
The EMI Group
Global Asset Management
Goldman Sachs International
Lazard Brothers & Co Limited
Linklaters & Alliance
Manpower PLC
Morgan Stanley Dean Witter
Nomura International plc
Nycomed Amersham plc
Robert Fleming & Co Limited
Schroder Investment Management UK Limited
Simmons & Simmons
UBS AG

**And Sponsors at
Tate Gallery Liverpool
and Tate Gallery of
Modern Art**

Liverpool
Corporate Members
BT
Hitchcock Wright and Partners
The Littlewoods Organisation PLC
Liverpool John Moores University
Manchester Airport PLC
Pilkington plc
QVC The Shopping Channel
Shell Research Ltd
Tilney Investment Management
United Utilities PLC

Tate Gallery of Modern Art
Ernst & Young

TateGallery

Pollo

This spring, the Tate hosts the first major Jackson Pollock show in Britain for 40 years and the largest retrospective of the great American painter's work ever assembled. The exhibition comes to London from the Museum of Modern Art in New York, where it opened last November to huge critical and public acclaim. Pollock's reputation has burgeoned since his death in a drunken car crash in East Hampton in 1955 at the age of 44. He is now widely acknowledged as the most influential American painter and a pivotal figure in the art of the twentieth century who developed a new way of painting, the echoes of which still reverberate today. In this extended section of *tate*,

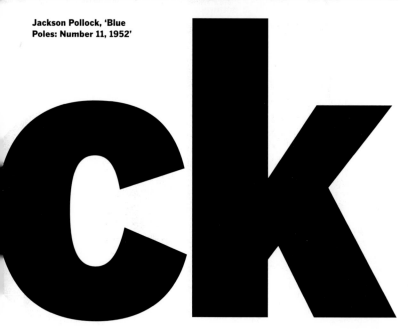

Jackson Pollock, 'Blue Poles: Number 11, 1952'

How Europe fell in love with Pollock

Jeremy Lewison on the painter's impact

It is hard to believe that it was only in 1955-1956, shortly before he died, that Jackson Pollock became something of a household name. Although his work had been seen in a few group shows in Europe from 1948 onwards, notably as part of Peggy Guggenheim's collection, by then housed in Venice, it was a series of exhibitions mounted by the International Council of the Museum of Modern Art, New York, that created his reputation. And what a reputation that was: "violent", "barbaric", "warpaint", "bomb", "decorative", "wallpaper", "liberated" were some of the words used to describe the man and his art. Wherever Pollock's painting was shown it caused a stir, whether in London, Paris, Berlin, Rome, Milan, Basel or Amsterdam. Many of the responses were based on misinformation provided by American critics keen to promote the myth of the virility of American art in the aftermath of the Second World War, a virility to match the diplomatic, political and military strength of the nation. They were also founded on the image of the introspective, macho male that Pollock permitted to be put out through photographs, film and personal statements. The time is now right to deconstruct some of those myths.

An examination of Pollock's reception in Europe must take into account not only the political, cultural and critical climate in each country, but also the mediation of Pollock through press coverage before his paintings were seen in actuality. In the space of this article it would be impossible to cover the whole of Europe, so I have limited myself to Britain, France and Italy, three countries which manifest substantial political and cultural differences in the post-war era. There are certain common attitudes, but also different emphases. The task is complicated by the fact that it is often difficult to disentangle responses to Pollock from those to Abstract Expressionism in general, because of the nature and number of exhibitions circulating in the 1950s.

Britain

The first mention of Pollock in Britain was in *Horizon*, edited by Cyril Connolly, which had established a reputation during the war as a lively, intellectual cultural magazine. In October 1947, Connolly devoted an issue to the United States which included Clement Greenberg's essay, "The Present Prospects of American Painting and Sculpture". This essay, I would argue, set the tone for the media's reception of the artist in Britain right up to 1958 when his retrospective took place at the Whitechapel Art Gallery. Greenberg claimed Pollock was the most powerful painter in America because he revealed himself through his art. "Gothic, morbid and extreme", "radically American", "violence, exasperation and stridency" are words he employs to champion the painter. Pollock and his fellow New Yorkers, Greenberg states, are engaged in "the ferocious struggle to be a genius".

Probably the next occasion that Pollock was brought to the attention of the English public was in the celebrated article in *Life* magazine in 1949, where he is pictured, as the text stated, "standing moodily next to his most extensive painting". Arnold Newman's photographs indicated

Jeremy Lewison examines the impact of Pollock and American Abstract Expressionism on Europe in the 1950s and reassesses the often violent critical and sometimes political responses. On page 29, Tim Marlow briefly charts the relationship between Pollock and film-makers, from Hans Namuth in the early 1950s to Hollywood now. On page 32, Ian Davenport, Martin Maloney, Helen Frankenthaler, Callum Innes and Julian Schnabel offer their own painters' perspective. Finally, on page 35, Michael Leja wrestles with the complex significance of figuration in Pollock's celebrated abstractions with his discovery of a group of virtually unknown paintings that Pollock dripped paint on to canvas laid on the floor, while the accompanying text mentioned that he employed unusual "non-art" materials. The description of Pollock's working methods promoted the accidental nature of his art, his responsiveness to his emotions and the activity of moving around the canvas.

Two years later, Jane Watson Crane, art editor of the *Washington Post*, identified Pollock in an article in *The Studio* magazine as one of the "progressives" who had "their roots in Cubism and Expressionism in its original sense" but who were developing an international abstraction. "The emphasis on Americanism," she wrote, "necessarily narrow and limiting, no longer exists to any recognisable degree."

These three articles adumbrate the four principal topics of the debate which was to take place in the British media, and indeed in the French and Italian newspapers: namely the savagery and violent nature of Pollock and his art, control versus accident, Americanness and the idea of "action painting". This last concept was, of course, first suggested in the pages of *Artnews* by the influential New York critic (and Greenberg's great rival) Harold Rosenberg in December 1952, shortly before Pollock's work first appeared in England in an exhibition entitled "Opposing Forces" at the ICA, but not one critic who reviewed this show appears to have been aware of Rosenberg's article. In fact, Rosenberg's ideas seem not to have filtered through to the British press until 1956. "Opposing Forces" was selected by Michel Tapié and Peter Watson and included the work of Sam Francis, Georges Mathieu, Henri Michaux, Alfonso Ossorio, Jean-Paul Riopelle and Iaroslav Serpan alongside three paintings by Pollock. Pollock's work arrived late, after a number of critics had reviewed the show. These critics, having absorbed the rumours about his method of painting, made light of the prospect of seeing his work. Those who attempted a more serious discussion were concerned that the works of these artists were nothing more than patterns. Critical appreciation of painting was still largely dependent on the theories of Roger Fry and Clive Bell. Only two critics reviewing the show, after the Pollocks were in place, perceived any difference between his paintings and those of his fellow exhibitors, and one of them, Patrick Heron, considered Pollock's work to be "mechanical".

By the middle of the decade the British public at large had seen nothing of Pollock other than in black and white reproductions. Thus, the impact of a large touring exhibition of contemporary American art which arrived in Britain in 1956 was considerable. "Modern Art in the United States", organised as a series of groupings beginning with what was termed the Older Generation of Moderns and ending with Contemporary Abstract Art, was the second-best attended show at the Tate since the war and was accompanied by two talks by Professor Meyer Schapiro, one a public lecture at the ICA on "Recent Abstract Painting in America", the other broadcast on the radio entitled "The Younger American Painters of Today", which was also published in the *Listener*. The exhibition was widely reviewed and, although the most popular paintings were by Andrew Wyeth and Ben Shahn, the greatest debate surrounded the contemporary section. Pollock was often held to typify his fellow abstract artists. Homer Cahill's introduction to the show lent credibility to some of the received views of Pollock which had been circulating ever since Greenberg's article in 1947. References to areas of the paintings "lassoed in [a] plunging gallop of line" and to Pollock slapping the canvas "with his paint-covered hands" merely compounded the view that he was some kind of Wild West savage. One critic referred to his paintings as "warpaint let loose", while Robert Stowe of the Communist *Daily Worker* described them as looking like the work of monkeys. The themes of bestiality, violence and barbarism were never far from many of the critics' minds. A slight variation was provided by John Russell in the *Sunday Times*. Headlined "Yankee Doodles", his inaccurate description of Pollock's painting procedures concluded: "I don't think that in this case it was the canvas that deserved the slaps", as though Pollock was a naughty child.

The level of debate was not particularly high. John Berger, who subscribed to an ideological programme in support of social realism, railed against Abstract Expressionism, contending that "these slashed, scratched, dribbled-upon, violated canvases [are not] worth taking seriously", thereby associating Abstract Expressionism with rape and destruction. Directing his bile at Pollock, he stated: "These works, in their creation and appeal, are a full expression of the suicidal despair of those who are completely trapped within their own dead subjectivity." For Berger, "action painting", as he now called it, had "nothing to do with art". There were, however, a handful of critics who welcomed Pollock warmly, if a little uncomprehendingly. Denys Sutton wrote an article in *Country Life* applauding the artist's attempts "to widen the range of creation by recourse to a kind of automatic painting" and looked forward to the time when it would be "enriched... by a deeper sense of humanism". Lawrence Alloway, who became the chief apologist for Abstract Expressionism in England in the 1950s, wrote, possibly in response to Sutton: "The tracks of these actions are not primarily decorative but charged with the humanity of the man who makes them." In *Arts*, Heron proclaimed that this exhibition had come at "the psychological moment... when curiosity about these painters", who had not been seen in London, "was keenest". He praised the size, energy, originality and invention of the works, but was concerned by what he described as Pollock's lack of understanding for "the pictorial science of colour" and his denial of space resulting from "the total absence of any strong planes".

One other theme preoccupied the critics in London, as it did in France; namely whether or not the paintings were specifically American. They felt that because many of the artists were born in Europe or had European ancestry, their work could be situated within the context of European movements. However, although the *Spectator*'s reviewer claimed that the work of Pollock, de Kooning and Rothko "should certainly not shock or surprise anyone familiar with abstract or non-figurative painting in Europe", he went on to concede that "for the first time... the United States has produced a body of painting which matches the scale and vigour of its technological enterprise and architectural expansion. In that sense the work is just as indigenous as that of the painters using a realistic language". Heron agreed that the movement was "specifically American [and] notably free of European influence", while Alloway remarked that in contrast to the American action painters, the Europeans "tend towards connoisseur type surfaces".

By the time the now legendary Pollock retrospective arrived at the Whitechapel in

Myths and legends. Pollock's 'Guardians of the Secret' from 1943

Tim Marlow on the love-hate relationship between Pollock and film

Lights, camera, action painting

In the summer of 1950, when Pollock was at the height of his artistic powers, a 35-year-old German *émigré* called Hans Namuth arrived at his East Hampton studio to take photographs of the painter at work. Although Pollock claimed to have finished the canvas he was working on – the now legendary 'One: Number 31, 1950' – once they went into the barn studio together, he "unexpectedly picked up can and paint brush and started to move around the canvas. His movements, slow at first," Namuth recalled, "gradually became faster and more dance-like as he flung black, white and rust-coloured paint on to the canvas."

The dozens of black and white photographs Namuth took that July afternoon would have been remarkable enough in themselves for future generations of art historians, but the photographer sensed that they didn't go far enough in capturing what he described later as "the flame of explosion when the paint hit the canvas". In fact, Namuth saw the possibilities for a different medium of documentation: "Pollock's method of working suggested a moving picture – the dance around the canvas, the continuous movement, the drama." And so, Namuth concluded, "to make a film was the next logical step".

Over the next few weekends, Namuth filmed Pollock in his studio in black and white and working away on an unstretched canvas which would later become 'Number 27, 1950'. About half of the resulting five minutes of film footage was shot overhead and the remainder from low on the floor. But Namuth was still unhappy with the results. "I realised that I wanted to show the artist at work with his face in full view, becoming part of the canvas, so to speak." The solution was simple but highly staged. Pollock would paint outside, where the light was stronger, and on to a large sheet of glass with Namuth filming underneath. The results were mesmerising, with Pollock performing his balletic dripping technique as if on to the surface of the film itself and with an expression of contorted concentration visible through the growing web of paint.

The consequences of Pollock's collaboration with Namuth were twofold. First, it triggered a return to drink for the painter, according to one of his biographers and friends – Jeffrey Potter – who was there when the filming finished. Allegedly, Pollock went straight into the house, grabbed a bottle of whisky and began slugging

Hans Namuth's photographs of Pollock at work on 'Autumn Rhythm: Number 30' in 1950

away after two years of not drinking a drop. Later that evening over dinner, Namuth and Pollock argued, with the artist apparently murmuring that the whole project had been "phoney" and ending the dispute by tipping up the dinner table. Pollock continued to drink heavily to the end of his life, five years later. Secondly, as Pepe Karmel points out in an extensive essay in the current exhibition catalogue, the films slowly but surely became central both to Pollock scholarship and in the burgeoning popular interest surrounding the artist and his life. He was the first major artist to be so extensively filmed at work and, as art historian Barbara Rose pointed out: "Namuth's photographs and films affected a far larger audience than the paintings ever had."

In turn, the films helped to fuel a potent Pollock mythology which has recently caught the attention of rather different kinds of film-makers,

Hollywood ones no less. Parallels between Pollock and movie stars such as James Dean (who also died in a car crash) and Marlon Brando have often been made, although Pollock himself was scathing. When asked what he thought about Brando's biker-boy performance in *The Wild One*, he replied: "What do they know about being wild? I'm wild. There's wildness in me. There's wildness in my hands." Over the past decade, a whole host of would-be wild boy actors (and the odd thespian) have been lined up to play the role of the wild artist.

The most glittering proposal dates from the early 1990s when Barbra Streisand bought the rights to Jeffrey Potter's Pollock biography, *To a Violent Grave*, and then hooked up with Tribeca Productions, owned by Robert De Niro who was set to play the part of the painter with Streisand as his wife Lee Krasner. Rumours that De Niro's parents knew Pollock well

were recently denied by the actor and the film project itself folded in 1996 after "creative differences".

Pollock's former lover, Ruth Kligman, who survived the fateful car crash in August 1956, wrote a memoir (called *Love Affair*) and subsequently a screenplay based on her short poignant time with the painter. Initially Al Pacino was interested in this, but recently Kligman told *tate* that she was still looking for financial backing and raised the idea of Kenneth Branagh playing the American action painter – an idea which seems closer to *Stella Street* than big-buck biopics.

An altogether more art-house affair has also been mooted with a screenplay by Mary Harron, who made *I Shot Andy Warhol*. Willem Dafoe was mentioned as a possible Pollock, with his partner Liz LeCompte as director. Following the success of *Basquiat*, painter-turned-temporary-director Julian Schnabel was also approached to direct a Pollock picture but "said no", as he told *tate* just before Christmas, "because I'm not interested in just making movies about artists".

Finally, a Pollock film is actually scheduled to be made this year, starring Ed Harris, who also makes his directorial debut. It stems from the Pulitzer Prize winning biography by Steven Niafeh and Gregory White Smith, extensively researched but with hefty doses of scandal rejected as scurrilous in certain quarters of the art world: not least the book's obsession with Pollock's supposed repressed homosexuality and his purported propensity for pissing, beginning with a memory of his father urinating on the rocks out west and culminating with the legendary episode when he doused Peggy Guggenheim's fireplace with his own particular animal scent. Quite whether Harris will transform *Time* magazine's idea of Pollock as Jack the Dripper to Jack the Pisser remains to be seen, but the signs are that he is taking the project seriously. Crucially, Harris has the goodwill of the Krasner-Pollock Foundation. He has spent time at the house and studio in East Hampton and has watched the Namuth films repeatedly. "Pollock's life was cinematic," the actor remarked recently. "Even the way he came to paint on the floor was cinematic." But the crux will be what kind of cinema the life and work are used to create. Pollock himself inadvertently threw down the real challenge to film-makers when he stated that "movies keep you outside looking outside. I want to look in, like a personality or soul x-ray".

November 1958 his name was widely known. Bryan Robertson, the gallery's director, made a special effort to accommodate the show. He successfully applied for a grant of £250 to modify the gallery, employing the architect Trevor Dannatt to design new internal walls and help to install the show. Robertson's intention was to hang the exhibition chronologically so that Pollock's development would emerge more clearly. He gave two lectures, both of which were sold out and at which Hans Namuth's film of Pollock painting was shown, while BBC television broadcast a programme on Pollock in the *Monitor* series.

The press reaction was considerably different from what it had been in 1956. Concern about the chaotic nature of his methods was replaced by recognition of an underlying sense of order. As Alloway remarked in *Art International*: "Faced with the huge, handsome exhibition… critics have dropped the myth of action and plumped for the myth of order." It was an epiphanic event for a number of critics who, for the first time, could see a large number of works, including drawings, presented in a broadly chronological sequence. That there were no early paintings, other than the more or less abstract 'The Flame', meant Pollock was presented in his most radical form. Yet so acceptable had he become that the critic of *The Times*, David Thompson, argued that "action painting", as exemplified by Pollock, "demands no judgments that would not apply in more conventional circumstances. Pollock's work immediately engages some measure or other of appreciative critical interest, and it is surely significant that the language of ordinary criticism remains relevant to it." Pollock, in other words, could be accommodated within the traditions of art. This review appeared very early on in the course of the show and set the tone for many of those which followed.

The myth of the violent savage was perpetuated in Sam Hunter's catalogue essay and continued to be espoused by some of the press. Even Alloway was not immune to it when he wrote in the *Listener*: "The paint has been showered down like a saturation bombing raid to produce an expressionistic tangle, recalling the violence of such earlier paintings as

'Male and Female'." Others, however, perhaps prompted by seeing Namuth's film, began to recognise a more gentle, rhythmic side to Pollock's art. There was still concern that his paintings were no more than decorations, and in an unprecedented third article in *The Times* about the exhibition, William Gaunt devoted his entire text to the problem: "What makes a painting decorative?"

The Whitechapel show laid the ground for the opening of "The New American Painting" in February 1959 at the Tate. The Abstract Expressionist movement as a whole was now well received by the majority of critics. John Russell recanted in his *Sunday Times* article, while Alloway, David Sylvester in the *New York Times* and the critic of *The Times* noted that New York had taken over from Paris as the centre for contemporary art. According to Alloway, European art was now academic. After the extensive coverage of the Pollock retrospective it was to be expected that he would not be singled out much in the reviews of "The New American Painting". Furthermore, the impact of Newman, who had not been seen in Britain, and Rothko was increasing. It appears that at the moment that Pollock reached his apogee, his star began to wane, although Bryan Robertson's monograph published in 1960 and an exhibition of the 'black pourings' at Marlborough Gallery in 1961 kept him in the public eye. The October 1958 article by Alan Kaprow, published in *Artnews*, in some respects paralleled the sentiments of many of the English critics that essentially Pollock's art was a dead end; while he might produce works of the highest quality, there was a limit to what could be said by using his methods. In the words of the *Burlington Magazine* critic, "no further development seemed possible".

Some critics remarked upon the countless Pollock imitators at the recent "Young Contemporaries" exhibition who, according to Sylvester, were "congenitally incapable of assimilating the intention" of the American school. Certainly, the immediate impact of Pollock on British artists was manifold and wide ranging. Alan Davie saw the work in 1948 in Venice. He was attracted by Pollock's interest in so-called "primitive" cultures and clearly impressed by the dripped works, as evidenced by the monotypes he made on his return from Venice. Davie had previously been attracted to the work of Paul Klee, Hans Arp and Joan Miró and his faith in the unconscious as an agent of liberation was rooted in his appreciation of their art. When he discovered Pollock he saw a kindred spirit. The monotypes are a blend of the influences of Pollock, Klee and Miró and have a very liquid feel, whereas his paintings of the 1950s manifest an interest similar to Pollock's for archetypes and suggestive symbols. Like Pollock, Davie had a fascination for Carl Jung.

British artists and critics were also impressed by the scale of painting coming from the United States. The exhibition "Place", held at the ICA in 1959 where Alloway was exhibitions organiser, included works which were placed on the floor to create environments. Many artists saw Pollock as a symbol of freedom, a precedent for doing whatever they liked in the name of action, regardless of whether or not they were in control of the medium. William Green chose to cycle over his bitumen

1920s

Paul Jackson Pollock is born at Watkins Ranch, Cody, Wyoming, on 28 January 1912. His parents are both of Scottish-Irish descent and Jackson is the youngest of five sons. Childhood is a migratory affair, with the family shifting between various small farms in Wyoming, Arizona and California.

In the summer of 1927, aged fifteen, Jackson works with a surveying crew near the Grand Canyon. He takes his first alcoholic drink and quickly gets a taste for it. By the beginning of winter he has joined the Reserve Officer

Training Corps at Riverside High School and been expelled for punching an officer while drunk on parade.

With an interest in art spawned by his oldest brother Charles, who had studied in both Los Angeles and New York by

The young Pollock in Los Angeles, c.1930

the time Jackson was sixteen and frequently wrote letters and sent his kid brother magazines and periodicals, Jackson enrolls at the Manual Arts High School in Los Angeles in 1928. Here, he first encounters abstract art and the mystical writings of Krishnamurti and Rudolf Steiner. Phillip Guston is a fellow pupil. After various disciplinary problems (including an involvement with the production of protest pamphlets), Pollock is expelled. Undeterred and following in his brother's footsteps, he leaves California at the age of eighteen to pursue an artistic career in New York in September 1930.

1930s

In his early years in New York, Pollock takes classes at the Art Students League and studies with the Regionalist painter Thomas Hart Benton, who both pushes Pollock to explore the work of the old masters and introduces him to mural painting. In turn, Pollock becomes captivated by the often brutally expressive work of the Mexican muralists: José Clemente Orozco, Diego Rivera and, in particular, David Alfaro Siqueiros, whose experiments with enamel paint and unconventional techniques, including

'Naked Man with Knife', 1938-1941

dripping, pouring and airbrushing, are seen first hand when Pollock assists him in his downtown Manhattan workshop.

As the Depression bites, Pollock finds work in the mural division of the

Federal Arts Project, part of Roosevelt's Works Progress Administration. From 1935 to 1938, he scrapes a living with the FAP but is effectively expelled for "continued absence". Having begun psychiatric treatment for alcoholism in 1937, he is hospitalised for three months in the summer of 1938. The best of Pollock's work which emerged towards the end of the decade is graphically violent and darkly erotic – in paintings such as 'Naked Man with a Knife' or 'Untitled (Woman)' – and shows a growing and original talent as well as a disturbed state of mind in the process of Jungian analysis.

Riding the Pollock line (clockwise from above): Alan Davie, 'An Elephant's Dream, 9 December 1948', 1948; William Green cycling over a canvas, 1958; Robyn Denny, 'Eden Come Home', 1957. Facing page: the Pollock exhibition at the Whitechapel Art Gallery, London, 1958

none more so than Anthony Caro. He left for America in 1959 as a figurative sculptor making bronzes in the expressionist tradition of Jean Dubuffet, Germaine Richier and Henry Moore and returned, having seen the work of David Smith and Richard Stankiewicz, to begin creating steel abstract sculpture. Encouraged by Clement Greenberg and a friendship with Kenneth Noland, he started to make highly colourful abstract sculptures, which sat on the floor rather than on a pedestal. While Caro credits Noland's practice of painting on the floor as having inspired this, Noland of course had picked up the habit from Pollock. Pollock's direct influence on Caro was relatively slight, but it seems inconceivable that such a work as 'Hopscotch', made by Caro in 1962, does not bear the memory imprint of 'Blue Poles', which was such a celebrated painting at the Whitechapel retrospective. Here Caro controls a horizontal field by means of a series of vertical or near vertical poles in the manner of Pollock's last great painting.

France

The earliest attempts to show Pollock in France were in the context of *informel* painting in exhibitions organised by Michel Tapié. He regarded Pollock as an exemplar of an internationalist "*art autre*", situated alongside *informel*, art brut and CoBrA, although he considered him an artist slightly apart, a "bomb" which he launched on to the Paris art

paintings. British artists also embraced destructiveness, perhaps taking literally the widely held view that Pollock was a destructive artist. Robyn Denny set fire to his paintings, which were paint-puddled in the manner of 'Yellow Islands'. Denny was one of a number of art students in the mid-1950s searching for something to replace the fly-blown idioms of the school of Paris. Having spent a period in Paris in the early 1950s, where he met a number of American students whose attitude towards French art was slightly irreverent, he became a rebellious student, first at St Martin's and then at the Royal College of Art. Although he was already something of an iconoclast, the arrival of American art in 1956 made a big impact on him. From now on, his gaze, like that of his contemporaries, was fixed on New York. During the years of austerity Britain seemed boring to a younger generation fed on images of America transmitted through films, television, music and art.

William Turnbull was one of the first artists to go to New York after the showing of "Modern Art in the United States". He had spent two years in Paris at the end of the 1940s, where he had first-hand contact with Alberto Giacometti, Constantin Brancusi, Jean Hélion, Fernand Léger and Tristran Tzara, and in the mid-1950s developed a style which reflected an interest in Jean Dubuffet and Nicholas de Stael. The 1956 show encouraged him in his pursuit of abstraction and to work on a larger scale. Shortly before departing for New York in 1957 he began producing a near monochrome type of painting, so he was immediately attracted to the work of Rothko and Clyfford Still. What he admired in these artists, and Pollock, was the materiality of the paint surface. He was also attracted to Pollock's ability to release an idea quickly, with assurance and without the self-consciousness he had detected in European *informel* painting. His trip to America showed him a more radical, instinctive approach to painting, but at the same time confirmed to him that his own roots were European.

Other artists, such as Gillian Ayres, were attracted to the surface texture of Pollock's paintings and worked with paint thinned with turps to achieve a sense of rich materiality. The explosive nature of her paintings had its origin in her admiration for both Pollock and *informel* painting.

It was not only painters, however, who changed direction after seeing the American shows in London. Sculptors, too, began to look west,

world. Pollock also found a strong supporter in Georges Mathieu, who regarded him, together with Wols, as a pioneer of non-figurative art. Indeed, Pollock's return to the figure in 1951 was something of a disappointment to Mathieu, who considered it imperative that artists should discover the means to communicate through a new system of signs. His articles of 1952 and 1953 were rare within French culture for their unreserved welcome and support for American abstraction. Interest in Paris was divided between the *informel* artists and those who remained wedded to geometry. Furthermore, the political situation in Paris was substantially different from that of London. The liberation of France by the Americans had left popular resentments as well as gratitude. At best the French were ambivalent about America. At worst they were hostile.

When "*Cinquante ans d'art aux Etats Unis*" arrived in Paris in 1955 American abstraction had enjoyed greater visibility in Paris than in London. Pollock had held a solo show at the Fachetti gallery in 1952 and had been selected for "12 Modern American Painters and Sculptors" at the Musée National d'Art Moderne in 1953. The 1955 exhibition, however, permitted the critics to assess the achievement of America over 50 years and, by and large, they did not refrain from attacking what they regarded as its provincialism, its dependency on Europe and its lack of native tradition. Sections of the press repeatedly noted the roots of American art in German Expressionism and decided the European origin of a number of the artists was conclusive evidence that American art did not exist. While it was safe to admire US architecture and film, painting, for so long the exclusive domain of Paris, was perceived as a threat. As for Pollock, he was rarely singled out for major discussion.

Four years later the Pollock retrospective and "The New American Painting" were shown simultaneously in Paris. They had been programmed very late in the day by Jean Cassou, the director of the Musée Nationale d'Art Moderne. Pollock dominated the reviews. His work had been extensively written about in *Cimaise* in 1956, where articles by Kenneth Sawyer and Julian Alvard highlighted the violent and destructive nature of his art. While he might have popularly been called the James Dean of painting by Georges Boudaille in the pro-Communist *Les Lettres Françaises*, there were increasing reports of his work being born of despair. Pierre Restany referred in 1959 to Pollock's "revolt" creating "the most remarkable kinds of excesses" and alluded to his "liberated anger". The reviewer of *Combat* described him as being "anxious to the point of despair". Individualism, violence, aggression and transgression were identified in his art, all characteristics of the vocabulary of Existentialism. Even Pollock's methods of working – self-expression before evaluation – could conform to Sartre's definition in *Existentialism and Humanism*: "We mean that man first of all exists, encounters himself, surges up in the world and defines himself afterwards." The notion of the suffering artist was also central to the existentialist view of art.

By 1959 Pollock was widely acknowledged in France as a formidable painter and chief among Abstract Expressionists. National primacy was less at stake and such critics as Michel Ragon could write that New York was not a province of the school of Paris but that an international language had emerged. There was as much movement across the Atlantic to New York as there was in the other direction. Moreover, as Pierre Imbourg wrote rather cheekily: "Pollock is the great painter of today... because he is dead" and therefore assimilable. Only reviewers from the papers of the extreme left and right, whose ideology could not accommodate so-called decadent art, refused to concede to Pollock's achievement, although even Boudaille in *Les Lettres Françaises* had to admit that his work was "not totally negative". *Cahiers d'Art*, which had been dismissive of American painting in the mid-1950s and had emphasised its European roots, published a long account of American abstraction by Dore Ashton in 1960.

As in Britain, Pollock had a considerable impact on the look of painting, which became increasingly gestural and large scale, and I believe two artists in particular owed him a considerable debt: Yves Klein and Niki de Saint Phalle. Klein's public performance in March 1960 at the Galerie d'Art Contemporain was memorialised on film and in photographs in a manner which I would suggest owes much to Namuth's film, which promoted art to the level of spectacle. There are many similarities between Namuth's editing and Klein's; for example, an emphasis on movement of body and hand and an interest in the materiality of paint and painting as a primal act. Where in Pollock's case the brush or stick is the phallus which empowers the artist to be creative – and you will recall Berger's reference to violation – in Klein's it is woman, whom he described as the "living brush", who is the instrument of power. Both artists rarely laid hands on their creations: conception was, so to speak, immaculate. We know that, in spite of his protestations to the contrary, Klein carefully controlled the look of his paintings. Niki de Saint Phalle could claim to have been more detached when she made the 'Shooting Pictures', inviting gallery visitors to fire a .22 rifle at plaster reliefs embedded with paint. These works accentuated the liquid appearance of paint and permitted the force of gravity to have a determining effect. Restany regarded them as parodies of American painting, particularly Pollock.

Italy

There were few reviews of Pollock in Italy before the retrospective took place in Rome in March 1958, but he certainly aroused interest among artists, notably Vedova and Fontana. Given the political context of postwar Italy, he provoked polarised if not wide-ranging views. In broad terms there was a tendency in Italy, more even than in France, for art to be seen to be at the service of politics. The Communists, following the lead given by Palmiro Togliatti, considered abstract art to be decadent, and espoused an art of social if not socialist realism as exemplified in the work of Renato Guttuso. Alongside it grew an increasingly active and vocal abstract movement which saw its roots in Futurism.

Italian artists, like Americans, had always suffered from being in the shadow of Paris, and when the new American painting burst on to the scene they shifted their place of pilgrimage from Paris to New York. Less schooled in the European tradition of abstraction – having been hindered in participating in it during the inter-war years because of the dominance of fascism – the Italians were more receptive to the Americans than the French had been. Allover painting seemed to have a link with Futurism in its dynamism, its chromatic power and its conception ▷

Painters on Pollock

Ian Davenport

My interest in Pollock began in my first year at college, when I was initially drawn by the myths surrounding him and his infamous reputation. However, as I began to discover more about the work, I realised just what an extraordinary artist he had been and was inspired to see the development from the early days to his artistic breakthrough with the classic drip paintings of the late 1940s and early 1950s. Pollock showed a way for me to bring disparate interests of my own together. Combining music, rhythm, sculpture and dance suddenly seemed inevitable, and a logical, natural way for a painting to exist. These elements could become the source and subject of a painting.

Often the most interesting work is made between one form of art or another, between sculpture and painting, dance and painting – in the space between the two. Pollock confirms this opinion. He was able to make art at the extreme limits of his medium's capability. I am amazed at how unapologetic and radical his work remains. A painting such as 'Lavender Mist' is undeniably beautiful, and I was struck by Pollock's apparent doubts about whether or not it was actually a work of art. Although there is incredible control and delicacy in such pieces, at certain times he is able to lose himself, becoming direct and passionate, which provides a wonderful pictorial tension. For myself, I was able to pick up certain aspects of his work and use these as a foundation to build upon. His use of materials, gravity and fluidity and the implied questioning of technique all suggested reconsidering the role of "thingness" and process.

Helen Frankenthaler

If I had to name any Jackson Pollock paintings that have particular meaning for me, they would include some of the work from the late 1940s and 'Lavender Mist' and 'Number 14'. Like any breakthrough artist, Pollock brought everything to bear on his process. He was "lost" in the making of his art; combining heart, mind, luck, innovations in method and materials and the *je ne sais quoi* that makes a gift magical and beautiful. In what ways did Pollock's work inspire me? Well, I was full of questions; his paintings were full of answers.

Martin Maloney

Large, expansive and raw, Jackson Pollock's paintings employed a democracy of method and materials which urged people to feel that anyone could have made them. In this respect, they were truly American. Pollock found a way to make work which says "Pollock was here" without using self-portraiture. He put himself in his painting through his inventive gesture. It's funny how we visualise his making method when looking at a work, which we don't do with any other artist. Looking at the paintings is like looking at a re-enactment of a performance. I admire the severity of his decisions; his limited colour, controlled spontaneity of gesture, the luxury of his indulgent repetition and practicality of using paint straight from the can of enamel. Pollock in all things was dedicated to being modern.

When I think of Pollock, I think of the Namuth photos of him in a T-shirt, looking like Brando, cigarette dangling, all muscles, sweat and method. He embodies the idea of the artist as hero, part pin-up, part tortured soul, flitting between poise and pose. Last summer I went to his studio and walked across the paint-splattered floor which is now an historic monument. I looked for the car crash site, I went to see his grave. Hard drinking, fast living, Pollock had an elegance in his calligraphic line which describes only itself. His gesture became an attitude for a new generation of artists trying to find how to describe the idea of an artist, the process of creativity and its place in their world.

© THE MUSEUM OF MODERN ART, NEW YORK. SIDNEY AND HARRIET JANIS COLLECTION FUND (BY EXCHANGE) © 1999 POLLOCK-KRASNER FOUNDATION, ARS, NY AND DACS, LONDON 1999

Callum Innes

Pollock has spanned and inspired different generations in a very interesting way. He epitomised all the painters of that period, as a hinge between the two halves of the century, creating this amazing body of work in such a short time. I have difficulty with some of his work, although it is incredibly powerful. There are major difficulties within it – it often walks a line on the edge of being overworked and decorative, of hardly being painting. He once asked Lee Krazner about one work – not whether it was good or bad, but whether it was painting. At some points the work seems to come together, to become his own. And you can still see all these difficulties, which is what makes it so interesting. That he epitomised the idea of the artist for the public is also interesting – having himself photographed in front of his paintings for *Life* magazine, while, of course, most artists' lives are much more mundane. This manipulation of image and the media was important, very much a precursor to what's happened here over the past ten years, and as such he can be seen as having been in the top flight of cultural modernity.

It is fascinating in the new show to see the radical shift from the early work influenced by Picasso and Surrealism to his poured paintings, yet there is always an undercurrent of drawing and subject from which he could never get away.

What's great about seeing 50 paintings together is that it throws all the problems into relief and you can see when the work is actually working; that is why it is so instructive to students today. There is constant evolution around a process, of development, of reassessment of influences, of restatement: almost going backwards to go forwards, to redress the balance. This can be seen in his three Black paintings of 1951, particularly 'Black Painting No 2', and in 'Summertime No 9A' or 'Black & White No 26A' of 1948, where he seems to readdress the element of drawing. It is the fallibility of his work that makes it intriguing.

Julian Schnabel

It's just great for young people, for old people, just for people that are interested in art to see a Jackson Pollock in the flesh, because you can't really tell a thing about it from looking at a photograph. Most great paintings you can't. I'd go and look at 'One' at MoMA and stand there for a while and watch the edges disappear, then let that whole thing start floating around and it would make me float around too. Those paintings fill you up, and that's what people really need to do: they need to empty themselves out and let paintings fill them up, instead of having so many ideas about it all.

I think that what he really wanted was to look in. The paintings look at you and you look at yourself looking at them, then your conscious intention disappears and you feel the effect of the interaction. That physical interaction between the object – being the painting – and the viewer is essential to the appreciation of this work. It's not a picture of something, it is something, a slice out of a bigger world. I think Pollock, in looking for an alloverness, didn't want to give you a rest. He wanted the painting to be relentless and never-endingly challenging you – taking you into that space without giving you something that would let up. Looking at Pollock's paintings we think about mark making and energy and some kind of transference from the rhythm of the world to the gesture of your body, and how to capture something that is expressive and simultaneously seems like it's not composed. That area where the pictorial and the objectness come together and you end up with magic. He was drawing with black and then he came back with white; there's silver, but there's a sort of skeleton of black that seems to be the stasis of his pictures.

It's said that among artists, some are cowboys and some are indians. Pollock was definitely an indian – I mean, even though he was a cowboy from out west, he was definitely an indian. Somebody like Vincent van Gogh was an indian – there was a kind of heat to the way they work. Georges Braque is a cowboy. Roy Lichtenstein is a cowboy. It doesn't make somebody good or bad, it's just that they're different types of people. I'm definitely an indian.

You can't say Pollock's name without thinking of the word "hero", because you've heard it so many times. What is a hero? Does a hero have to die from hubris? I think he had some real highs and some real lows, and we are the beneficiaries of the highs and he was the recipient of the lows.

Pollock's 'Number 14, 1951', 1951, and (top) 'One (Number 31, 1950)', 1950

of the painting as a field of energy. Furthermore, the arrival in Rome of Rothko, Kline, Twombly and de Kooning in the late 1950s brought first-hand contact with Abstract Expressionism.

When the Pollock show opened in Rome, preceding "The New American Painting" in Milan by a few months, Pollock was already a known artist. Yet the reviews of the Roman press did not differ substantially from those of Britain. The Latin temperament perhaps encouraged them to write even more exaggeratedly about the wildness and violence. The conservative *Il Tempo* wrote of "feverish obsession", "furious lyricism" and "frenzied desire", while its sister paper, under the headline "The volcanic Pollock", talked of "flashing and barbaric apparitions" and "convulsed screams". James Dean and Elvis Presley were comparators for the populist press. The left-wing party organs tended to come out against Pollock, whom they considered to be representative of a decadent culture, summoning up all the clichéd views of American life to condemn him. There were, however, one or two important exceptions. The *Corrispondenzi Socialista* commented that this was an important exhibition and noted that even if the Communists had not liked it, they had taken it seriously enough to review it. (The Communists and the socialists were by no means united in their cultural views.) The most astonishing article, however, appeared in the pro-Communist *Paese Sera* by Marco Venturoli. Explaining that he and fellow Communists were generally against abstraction, because it was meaningless and merely decorative, he confessed: "Though we still believe that in the great part we were right, faced with the retrospective exhibition of Pollock… we feel it our duty to modify our former position; we do this with great satisfaction, as an act of homage to art which is capable of modifying any *parti pris*, no matter how legitimate. Yes, Pollock is a painter and he is an artist; it is impossible not to accept his formidable and indubitable results. Above all we must confess to having erred in one of our critical premises; this is, that nowadays one could not paint or create sculpture without at least some reference to external reality."

The importance of this should not be underestimated. It was not a change of view in the order of John Russell's, which was essentially with the tide of opinion. Venturoli's *volte face* struck at the very heart of Communist ideology within a Communist Party organ and did not go unnoticed by at least one fellow journalist. Giovanni Russo, in the Milanese independent newspaper *Corriere d'Informazione*, gave a gleeful account of the event and concluded: "Is it not instructive that an American artist, and an abstract one at that, has been able to bring confusion and crisis into the ranks of our Communist conformists who have so exalted that brand of social realism which is imposed by the artists of the Soviet Union?" Essentially, the Pollock show was a double blow: not only did it undermine the exclusive belief in social realism, but it indicated that a capitalist culture could produce great art.

The impact of Pollock on artists was also considerable. Ever since the early 1950s there had been a growing interest in gestural abstraction and such artists as Emilio Vedova moved away from Futurist-derived, geo-

Italian rhythm and French fire power. Left: Emilio Vedova in his studio, Rome, 1958. Below: Niki de Saint Phalle, 'Shooting Picture', 1961

metric abstraction towards a free-flowing variety. Namuth's film clearly made an impression as can be seen in photographs of Vedova at work in the early 1960s. More interesting than this, however, was the impression Pollock made on the artists who would become associated with Arte Povera. Jannis Kounellis has acknowledged that in the making of 'Untitled 1968', recently acquired by the Tate, he was thinking of 'Blue Poles'. Its sense of organic growth and horizontal expansion, its "dripping" wool held in check by two strong vertical elements, are highly reminiscent of Pollock's painting. And Michelangelo Pistoletto has stated that he began to make mirrored works to investigate the problem, which he perceived Pollock never resolved, of how to enter into a painting rather than allowing it an autonomous existence. Pistoletto was one of many European artists whose work began to incorporate the body, an interest which I believe came out of the impact of Pollock and Namuth's photographs.

The exhibitions of Pollock's work in these three countries, as elsewhere in Europe, undoubtedly had a huge impact. Whether positively or negatively, scarcely a movement in the 1960s was not in some way or another spawned by a reaction to his art and method of addressing the canvas. Painterly pop, post-painterly abstraction, minimalism, Arte Povera, op art, gestural abstraction, performance art, conceptual art and installation art can all be related back to Pollock. Forty years later, painting is taking something of a back seat in the face of interest in new technology, and, ironically, Pollock is treated like an old master. But the power of his art is such that it still looks radical and I would not mind betting that, as a result of the Pollock exhibition at the Tate, painting may well come back into fashion.

1940s

At the beginning of 1940, the Museum of Modern Art stages a large Picasso retrospective, which has a big impact on Pollock. The following year, he sees "Indian Art in the United States" at MoMA and watches Navajo Indians execute poured sand paintings on the gallery floor.

Nineteen forty three sees Pollock in a group exhibition at Peggy Guggenheim's newly founded Art of this Century gallery, which, for the next five years, becomes a major force in the promotion and development of what is later termed the New York School. Piet Mondrian encounters Pollock's paintings and is impressed, notably by 'Stenographic Figure'. "I think this is the most interesting work I've seen so far in America," Mondrian tells Guggenheim, "You must watch this man." She obliges with a contract of $150 a month and a solo show for Pollock at the end of the year. She also commissions him to do a mural for her town house. In his excitement, he rips down a wall in his house to stretch the 20ft canvas. His emotional life becomes more stable as he establishes a relationship

'Stenographic Figure', c.1942

with painter Lee Krasner. At the end of 1945, the two of them go to live in a farmhouse on Long Island at The Springs, East Hampton. Initially, there is no hot water or bathroom, but Pollock's work

continues to develop. "Drinking or not, he never got up in the morning," Krasner recalled. "While he had his breakfast I had my lunch… He would sit over that damn cup of coffee for two hours. By

that time it was afternoon. He'd get off and work until it was dark. There were no lights in his studio. When the days were short he could only work a few hours, but what he managed to do in those few hours was incredible."

From the end of 1947, Pollock begins to pour and drip paint on to canvases placed on the floor of his barn studio, using dried out brushes, sticks or cans of paint with holes in them. To emphasise their abstract qualities, he titles the works only with numbers and years.

Clement Greenberg proclaims Pollock to be "the most powerful painter in contemporary America", and in August

1949, *Life* magazine responds with a half-mocking, half-incredulous six-page feature headed: "Is he the greatest living painter in the United States?" Pollock becomes America's first post-war art "star".

'Free Form', 1946

Michael Leja on the complex significance of a group of little-known paintings
Pollock reframed and refigured

Among the dazzling paintings gathered in the "Jackson Pollock" exhibition is a small group that may seem a peculiar departure from the artistic logic visible all around it. This handful of paintings hung together at MoMA in a room set between the early (1947) explorations of Pollock's infamous process (pouring and flinging paint on to a canvas laid out on the floor) and the monumental canvases of 1950 that mark the culmination of his labours in this mode. Dating from 1948 and 1949, the works are distinguished by a surface that has been dramatically disrupted, either through cutting out some part of it or pasting on to it a piece of another painting. Moreover, the dislocated parts are distinctly figurative, resembling the playful conglomerations of body parts Picasso and the Surrealists devised years earlier. In these two respects – overt figuration and excision or collage – the paintings are unique among the works from Pollock's "classic" period included in the exhibition. But their apparent eccentricity in the context of the show is deceptive.

The reunion of these few paintings, gathered from Canada, Japan, Germany and other undisclosed locations, provides an extraordinary opportunity to observe Pollock systematically experimenting with the possibilities for merging figurative forms with abstract linear fields. Whether he was seriously interested in this problem and what significance it should have for our understanding of his greatest abstract

Masterly miasma. Pollock's 'Out of the Web: Number 7, 1949', 1949

paintings are questions that have long fired debates among Pollock scholars. The artist spoke of choosing to "veil the image" in one painting, and on another occasion he noted that "when you're painting out of your unconscious [as he believed he was, to some extent], figures are bound to emerge". But, on the other hand, he also said "abstract painting is abstract", and he numbered rather than titled most of his abstract paintings to discourage Rorschach responses. For some interpreters, whatever play of figuration there may be in the abstract paintings is of little consequence; for others, it is essential to understanding Pollock's art.

The paintings with ruptured surfaces show Pollock experimenting with different ways of merging figure and field. In 'Untitled (Cut Out)', for example, a flat-headed figure with crudely articulated limbs and torso has been cut from the centre of a cardboard panel covered over with a thickly painted, multi-coloured field accented with shards of coloured glass and dominated by a network of crisscrossing cords of orange, blue and ochre paint. Nothing in the tangle of lines and marks anticipates the form of the figure; it was once an indistinguishable part of the painting and has materialised only in the process of being extracted. To keep the figure from being simply a hole in the painting, a white canvas panel with a few apparently haphazard markings serves as backing. During some of the time that the painting remained in Pollock's studio, however, the figurative hole was left open. Photographs indicate that Pollock hung the picture in this state in 1950, when it was tacked to the wall next to 'One: Number 31, 1950', witnessing the production

of the large-scale poured works of that year, such as 'Autumn Rhythm' and 'One'. In that state the planks of the barn wall showing through lent material presence to the figure, the wood grain perhaps suggesting surrealist frottage; but the persistent legibility of the planks as "wall", continuous with the field surrounding the painting, enforced awareness of the absence at the centre of the panel.

It is likely that Pollock used 'Cut Out' in this open form in the production of other works. He made two paintings on paper in late 1948 or early 1949, one of which, 'Figure', is in the exhibition, and they echo its shape so closely that the paint was probably poured through 'Cut Out', using it as a stencil to guide the paint stream. Pollock's hand was steady: the meandering black enamel line poured on to the white ground is largely continuous and punctuated with spots and pools, two of which fix the eyes, but it is never marred by contact with the stencil. 'Figure' is a simple painting with remarkable features: a contained and controlled yet undirected and impulsive line passively describes a body without employing conventional techniques of delineating boundaries, contours, or structural elements. It differs from the other paintings with which it is grouped in having a monolithic surface, but its form gives evidence of the double surface involved in its production. At some point Pollock tried filling the hole in 'Cut Out' with a backing quite different from the one it now has. A studio photograph from around 1949 shows Lee Krasner standing in front of the painting, which hangs on a white wall. A black backing

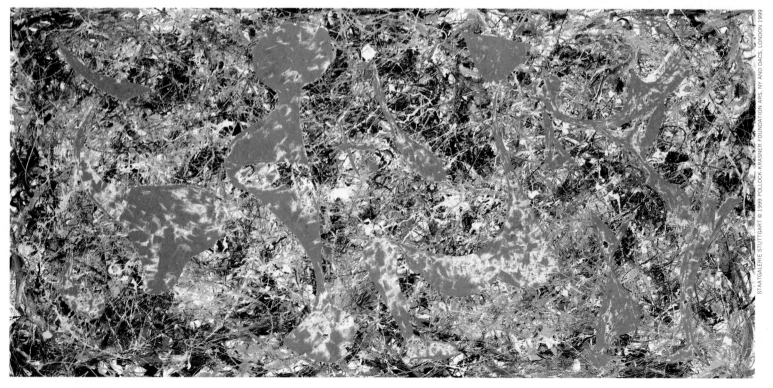

partially covered with a light linear field, lighter than the overall tonality of the surrounding painting, shows through the opening. Pollock here seems to be seeking an alternative to stark separation between figure and ground, testing what happens when the distinction between them is one of colour and tonality across similar linear fields. Apparently he was dissatisfied with this solution, since the dark backing was removed by 1950.

By the time of Pollock's death in 1956, the hole in 'Cut Out' had been filled by a white field partly smeared with patches of ochre, black, crimson and aluminum paint. These markings are so dispersed and casual that the panel seems a found object. The accidents that account for them and allow them to show through the overlaid panel suggest a form of chance more extreme than the accidental splashes and splatters that make up the surrounding field. Yet some of them have a surprising aptness, such as the aluminum arc across the bottom of the panel which reads, through the cut out, as bands across the figure's ankles. The strong presence of aluminum pourings in the surrounding tangle makes these bands seem to extend out from it to hold the figure and bring it up or pull it back to the surface of the painting. All the marks on the white backing work to smooth but preserve the disjunction between figure and linear field in the painting, which makes it easier to believe that Pollock may have

intended this solution to be the definitive conclusion to his extended experimentation with this painting. Uncharacteristically, he left it unsigned and undated, which gives cause to wonder whether he ever considered it complete. None the less, the balanced tension between presence and absence and between integration and disintegration in 'Cut Out' suggests detachment, alienation, containment and ensnarement – enduring themes in the interpretation of Pollock's work.

The figure cut from the centre of 'Cut Out' became the core of a second work, 'Untitled (Cut-Out Figure)', in which it stands at the centre of a dark ground virtually identical in size to the panel of which it was originally part. The pourings and markings the form acquired as part of the field of 'Cut Out' apparently have not been changed; if restored to its original location, the markings would match up line for line. The original painting's surface encrustation is thickest within the figure, especially in the region of the abdomen, where unrecognisable materials, perhaps nails and pebbles, complement the pieces of coloured glass embedded in the paint. The tubular crisscrossing lines, either squeezed from a tube or more likely poured using quite thickened paint, cross the figure at all angles and disappear at its edge. In this arrangement their resemblance to cords is reinforced as they seem to lace the figure to the black ground on which it has been placed.

A broad flat band, like a wide shoelace covered with paint, crosses the chest diagonally and adds to the suggestion of bondage. The black ground surrounding the figure has been marked with off-white linear pourings which blanket the field in one layer of uniform density. (When the companion painting 'Cut Out' was temporarily superimposed on a black field with light pourings it constituted a strict reversal of 'Cut-Out Figure'.) These lines venture into all the varied peninsulas between the appendages of the figure, but always stop short of its pronounced edge. With a few minor exceptions, the pours do not violate these boundaries, although similar cream-coloured lines and pools are visible among the layers of pourings that compose the figure.

The figure-ground dynamic in 'Cut-Out Figure' is further complicated by the figurative presences outlined in the heaviest pours at the right and left of the collaged humanoid. These bodies, which are comparable in size to the central figure, face inward towards it and seem engaged in an exchange of attention or gesture with it. Together the three figures structure a composition that resembles several of Pollock's earlier paintings in which sentinels flank a centred motif (such as 'Guardians of the Secret', 'Pasiphae' and 'The Key'). Recognition of the flanking figures is delayed and uncertain; they emerge slowly and tentatively from the seemingly abstract poured lines, revealing some measure of deliberate control, guiding marks that initially seem random. The painting's two models of figuration confront one another: poured lines actively forming figures are juxtaposed with poured lines constituting a field made figurative through a second shaping operation. The linear network within the collaged figure becomes striking for its lack of an organising principle, and Pollock's ability to use the poured line with more or less direction and control is highlighted.

The collaged figure, then, is doubly pinned into its new location: its internal paint cords bind it to its new ground, and it anchors a grouping of heterogenous figures arrayed across the panel. The original rupture produced by the addition of the collage element is mended in these ways, but spatially the painting remains disunified, with figure and ground locked in an unstable vacillation. The collaged figure alternately lurches forward and is drawn back depending in part on whether recognition of the poured figures is activated or suspended. Again, Pollock has generated a tense dynamic of integration and disintegration, of figuration and abstraction.

Another pair of works from about the same time was generated by the same excision/collage process – 'Rhythmical Dance' and 'Untitled' from 1948 – but with some noteworthy variations. In this pair, the figures are smaller and de-centred; furthermore, their limbs and torsos have been so attenuated that

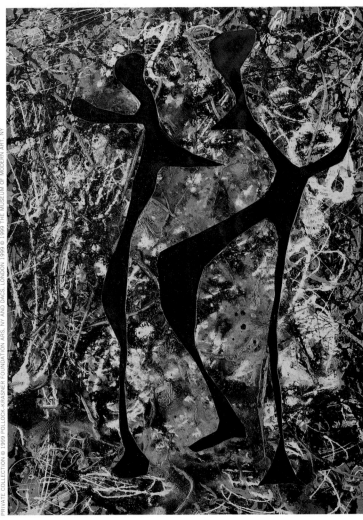

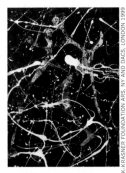

Left: Pollock's little known and previously unpublished work, 'Untitled (Rhythmical Dance)', from 1948 and, above, its pictorial counterpart, 'Untitled', 1948

they merge more harmoniously with the poured linear fields, almost as if they were simply aggregates of especially heavy pours. Their forms are evocative of Picasso's surrealist dancers and bathers of twenty years earlier; like those prototypes, and partly as a result of invoking them, their gestures can be read as simultaneously desperate and playful.

In 'Rhythmical Dance', a painting which to my knowledge has not been exhibited in decades and whose location was unknown until MoMA's curators recently discovered it (too late to be reproduced in the catalogue and not, alas, travelling to London), layers of cream, black and aluminum pourings, accented with thick ropes of ochre, yellow and orange, have been applied to a sheet of paper coloured reddish brown. At the top and sides of the picture, these components are sharp edged, but at the centre and bottom, all are blurred together as if splashed with solvent. Pebbles have been sprinkled over this surface, and most of the cords of warm colours have small pebbles embedded in them at regular intervals. These paint cords are thicker and more pronounced than those in 'Cut Out', but the surface overall is less thickly encrusted. From this sheet two narrow figurative forms have been cut, and a smooth black backing has been attached. In the midst of so much tactile variation, the cut edges of the figures could be relatively inconspicuous, but the evenly painted and untextured black of the backing contrasts sharply with the materiality of the poured surface. The excised figures are conglomerations of appendages, sometimes of unspecifiable identity. The figure on the right contains an arm (or breast) that points towards the upper right corner and is cut from the centre of a circular cream pool. Otherwise, the forms of the figures bear no obvious relation to the painted marks. They are, however, decoratively, harmoniously and evenly disposed in the field.

In the untitled pendant, however, the effect is quite different. The collaged figures have been positioned differently on the black ground. The one on the left leans towards the

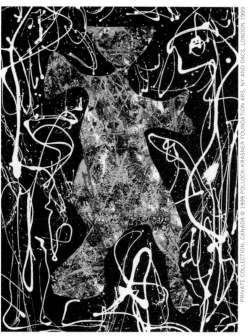

Flipping the figure. 'Untitled (Cut-Out)', c.1948-1950, (above left) and 'Untitled (Cut-Out Figure)', 1948

centre of the composition; the one on the right has been rotated slightly counterclockwise. As a result they appear much more unstable, their appendages are even less easily identified and their forms now suggest loss of balance or disorientation. While some paint cords imported on the figures do bind them to the ground, as in 'Cut-Out Figure', the differences from the latter work are more striking. The figures have been literally enmeshed by the new pourings. The cream lines that constitute the painted field here pass over them in trajectories that seem largely undetermined and uninterrupted by the figures they contain. Some parts of the figures are circled by paint loops. For example, the left leg of the one on the right is targeted by one poured loop; this figure is also lassoed around the waist. Embedded in the poured web and positioned as if suspended or ensnared, they literalise themes of entrapment and entanglement. The web of pourings that constitutes the collaged figures is in dialogue with the tangle that is the encompassing field. Within and without, the figure is formed and immersed in fields and processes in which

directedness and impulse, control and uncontrol do battle.

By far the largest and most complex of the works with ruptured surfaces is 'Out of the Web: Number 7, 1949', whose title makes explicit the metaphor invoked in my descriptions above. After the application of paint was completed, Pollock used a knife or razor blade to incise shapes into the masonite surface; then, with a chisel, he removed the surface within the incised boundaries. The process of removal was violent and labour intensive; it is sometimes mistakenly described as a matter of "peeling off" the paint layer, when in fact the surface makes clear that extraction involved gouging and hacking. The exposed masonite is deeply scarred from the violence of removing the figures. The process was obviously laborious, or at least it was made to look so. Much of the scraping was done with the side of the chisel, leaving deep ridges and occasionally revealing at the edges of the forms a neat cross section of the paint layers. In some of the scraped out forms, bits of the paint surface have been left,

1950s

The myth of the tough guy dressed in black denim with a casually held cigarette is circulated to a mass audience via *Life* magazine, but images of Pollock at work also arouse widespread curiosity. "On the floor I am more at ease," Pollock explained in a widely quoted statement. "I feel nearer, more a part of the painting, since this way I can walk around it, work from all four sides and literally be in the painting... I continue to get further away from the usual painter's tools... When I am in my painting, I'm not aware of what I'm doing. It is only after a sort of 'get acquainted' period that I see what I

'Yellow Islands', 1952

have been about."

In the late summer and early autumn of 1950, Pollock produces what have since been called his most "classical" drip paintings, three vast canvases measuring roughly nine by eighteen feet: the aggressive and monochromatic 'Number 32, 1950'; the softer, dense and intense 'One: Number 31, 1950'; and the

balletic, lyrical brown white and black web of the great 'Autumn Rhythm: Number 30, 1950'. He is filmed and photographed painting parts of the last two pictures by Hans Namuth which has a huge impact on the continuing mythologisation of Pollock, "the all-American Action Painter". More immediately, however, it triggers off a bout of heavy drinking after two years of abstinence and Pollock subsequently plunges into deep depression.

Over the next two years, Pollock produces dark, brooding "poured" paintings, where black paint is poured and stained on to the canvas and in which figurative

imagery seems to resurface. But his output grows increasingly small as the drinking gets more acute; after a flourish with the vast 'Blue Poles' in 1953, only the odd, isolated picture emerges.

In the summer of 1956, after two traumatic years, Lee Krasner takes a break and travels to Europe. Pollock has an affair with a young artist called Ruth Kligman, who temporarily moves to The Springs. On 11 August, Pollock, Kligman and her visiting friend Edith Metzger go on the fateful road trip that ends in carnage when the drunken Pollock hits a tree at 10.15pm. Kligman survives, but Metzger and Pollock are killed.

Figuring a route into abstraction. Pollock's epic early work 'Mural' from 1943. Below right: Pollock working on a painting on glass, 1950. A still taken from the film by Hans Namuth and Paul Falkenberg

as if too resistant to be overcome. Elsewhere, the masonite is white or brown: where the scraping is shallow, traces of the white ground and even some surface colour remain visible; where the gouging is deep, only the brown matter is exposed. Some of the cut-out figures are completely discrete, while others have open sides that allow the painted field to bleed in. Liberation from the surface web apparently has entailed some cost to the integrity of the figures. The difficulty of extraction has been made part of the picture's surface. The figure on the middle right evokes Picasso's squatting demoiselle d'Avignon; her back is turned towards the viewer and, in Pollock's version, her foot points improbably inward. The two large figures at the left are strongly Miróesque – one humanoid, the other biomorphic. The one on the right seems to be running or falling towards the left. The contours of these forms are elegant and fluid; they produce a rhythmic, even balletic formal movement proceeding from right to left. This formal elegance in the drawing of the figures, dominant when the painting is viewed from a distance, contrasts sharply with the tortured facture visible at close range. Approach and

withdrawal provide partial and contradictory readings, and, through the disparity, the picture unites the harmonious grace of 'Rhythmical Dance' with the disjunctive figure-field relations of 'Cut Out'. Here again, a ruptured surface and composition are counterweighed by unifying effects.

Web imagery is present at many levels in the picture – in the texture of the masonite, highlighted in some areas by the drag of a dry brush across it; in the grey cross-hatchings prominently brushed into the wet surface; in the overall tangle of poured lines that dominates the field. At each level, metaphors of containment and release are effected by the carved-out figures. What makes this work different from the previous examples is the prominent staging given to labour and violence in the process of extraction. Cutting into a rigid material is an activity significantly different from cutting out a soft one. One difference is that here the support is not perforated; the literal depth of the masonite panel as ground is invoked. This actual ground carved out as figures competes for the status of "ground" with the surrounding painted areas. When figures lodge such an assertive claim to being the true ground of the painting, familiar figure-ground relations are subverted. Another difference is that the destructive aspects of the effort to combine

figure and field in the cut and collaged works are foregrounded in 'Out of the Web'. As a result, the artist's presence and his role in the production of the image are highlighted and take on new significances. Pollock is revealed as producer of both delicate and violent gestures: in the first stage he generates the dense, entangling web that is the painted field; then he constitutes figures within that web through a traditional process of automatic drawing with a non-traditional tool – a knife; and finally, he liberates those figures through vigorous scraping and hacking. This multi-stage process is exceptionally suited to allowing Pollock to enact and symbolise the interplay of control and uncontrol that is an insistent theme of his work. 'Out of the Web' invites us to recognise the contradictory character of the actions required to produce it. At the same time, it offers us an image of figures wrought in conflict, simultaneously trapped and liberated, and whose violent and laborious liberation can be no more than imperfect given their internal permeation by the web. Extraction has left a battered and scarred shadow, half in and half out, with residue of the internal web visible throughout. Implicit in the painting are ideas about the individual and the human situation that had wide currency in the US when Pollock was painting. In the wake of the traumas of the

figuration is concealed in the dense tangle of marks, although sometimes it is left unmistakably apparent. One wonders why the selection of paintings in the show does not more fully represent both alternatives.

The exhibition itself wants to make a somewhat different point about the paintings of the 1947-1950 period. It highlights the sophistication, subtlety and variation in Pollock's handling of individual marks and overall compositions. This is certainly a worthy argument, and it is well made by the remarkable variations of part and whole evident in the paintings gathered. Pollock clearly mastered his seemingly unmasterable process and made it yield a surprising range of lines, marks and compositions at will. But he also insistently injected disturbances and disruptions into his paintings to counterweigh their formal coherence and to undermine any impression they might give of purely masterful control. Figuration paradoxically signified Pollock's control of his medium at the same time that it functioned to disrupt the allover abstract order of many of his paintings. I find curious the desire of some Pollock admirers to filter it out or to limit its significance. Even Karmel, in the end, wants to restrict Pollock's figuration to service as a supplier of dynamism to the abstract compositions: "The rhythmic energy that animated Pollock's work at every level, from the individual line to the overall composition… seems in large part to have resulted from the interaction between Pollock's figurative imagery and his allover, all-absorbing web." This is no doubt true, but the significance of figuration extends beyond formal dynamics. The web was not always as allover and all-absorbing as the selection of paintings in the exhibition implies. Figuration is part of a fundamental impulse towards heterogeneity in the classic paintings, and it can be recognised and interpreted without reducing Pollock's paintings to occasions for Rorschach projections. Recognising its insistent engagement with figuration does not close down but rather opens up Pollock's work.

Appreciating the complex significance of figuration in Pollock's art brings many advantages. It builds bridges to the more overtly and consistently figurative earlier and later work, it admits metaphorical responses that he himself encouraged in some of his statements and titles (for example, 'Out of the Web') and it facilitates broad recognition of the complex and contradictory interests that motivated his painting. Moreover, by enlarging the sphere of unruliness in Pollock's great abstractions, it discourages reductive readings of them as, above all, solutions to formal or procedural problems. Figuration is like all the heterogeneous ingredients of Pollock's trademark paintings: it is a factor in both method and meaning.

"Jackson Pollock", Tate Gallery, London, 11 March-6 June

1930s and 1940s, an image of human beings as trapped between uncontrollable dark impulses and the entanglements of cosmic fate held considerable explanatory power.

Although not included in the exhibition, there are other important paintings by Pollock from this period conjoining figuration and ruptured surfaces ('Wooden Horse' and 'Shadows' are reproduced in the catalogue) which indicate that such interests concerned him throughout his period of greatest productivity between 1947 and 1951. The experiments with 'Cut Out' alone extended well across these years. What the exhibition excludes, however, are paintings containing clearly figurative pourings on continuous and unified grounds. Their absence may give visitors the impression that Pollock explored figuration only in conjunction with excision and collage, and that the group of works in which these combined interests were developed constituted a strange experimental offshoot separate from the more important abstract paintings. Those who have read the catalogue essay by Pepe Karmel will not make this mistake. Karmel's close examination of the complete collection of Hans Namuth's famous photographs and films of Pollock at work – only a small fraction of which had been released before now – generates a strong argument for the importance of figuration in even the most abstract of Pollock's paintings. Assembling the photographic record chronologically, and using digital manipulation to rectify and combine some of these images, Karmel reconstructs as much as possible the layer-by-layer evolution of some of the great abstract paintings of 1950. He demonstrates persuasively that the first stages of 'Number 27, 1950' and the last additions to 'One: Number 31, 1950' contain clear figurative drawing, and, moreover, that Pollock's typical procedure apparently involved alternating figurative with abstract campaigns: there were intervals of semi-controlled drawing with poured paint amid the violent flinging in the production of the best documented paintings. Usually the

After three years of political wrangling Rachel Whiteread's Holocaust memorial will finally be constructed in Vienna later this year. Meanwhile, the British sculptor has continued to develop as a major international artist, winning a prize at the 1997 Venice Biennale and receiving rapturous reviews in New York for 'Water Tower', her first outdoor public work since 'House'. In a revealing interview with David Sylvester, Whiteread talks about her recent work, her plans for a plinth in Trafalgar Square and her discovery of a previously unrecognised affinity to the art of carving

Carving

David Sylvester: *I'd like to ask you what art by others has especially interested you.*

Rachel Whiteread: It might mean talking about my work as well.

The more the better.

When I was a student at Brighton, I was a painter initially, and in the last year of my degree course I realised that I just wasn't interested at all in painting. In the first year I'd been making paintings that were on canvas, and in the second year I'd started making things that came off the wall. In the third year I was casting things and making installations using lines and rubber tubes, bits of old stuff found on the beach. I was very naive, and at that time I was certainly looking at American art, particularly Eva Hesse and Jackie Windsor and people like that. I then went to the Slade to study sculpture, and I almost didn't want to have too much information from other artists, because I just felt I hadn't found a way through myself. I had teachers such as Antony Gormley and Alison Wilding and Eric Bainbridge, and they were all the young stars who were teaching me at Brighton and then at the Slade. I think they could see things in my work that I couldn't see at that point. Someone like Ed Allington told me to go and see this Louise Bourgeois show years ago at the

Serpentine and I was absolutely blown away by it. Then I also started coming to see shows at d'Offay's, and there was a Nauman show at the Whitechapel. I hadn't done much travelling. I had never been to America at that point, so it wasn't as if I was desperately trying to find this way through American art, but I think it was actually the Americans who were influential: people such as Carl Andre and Serra. I was certainly looking at minimalism and at things that were making art out of nothing, starting with a lump of metal or something. But I was also very interested in Piero della Francesca and Vermeer and painters whose work was absolutely about silence. I suppose that one develops a language, and that's what has continued the development of the work rather than looking at other artists.

You found your own language at an early age.

Well, I remember when I was leaving college and made my show at the Slade. I hid it really. I showed it in the metal workshop and everything was hidden underneath things and behind doors. A lot of people didn't actually see it. I think I didn't really feel ready to show in some ways. And all the work was very autobiographical, and a lot of it was quite sad. So I left the Slade and took on a studio and sat on my own for a year and cried and stared at the wall, or whatever it is I did, totally unable to make anything substantial. There was a woman called Barbara Carlisle, who'd seen my show at the Slade and gave me an exhibition in Islington. She had a small gallery, and I think it was just someone putting faith in me and saying: "Yes, I think what you're doing's interesting." It made me focus and I made the very first piece of sculpture that I ever made, really, 'Closet', which was the cast of the inside of a wardrobe covered in black felt. It was based on a sort of childhood experience, and I remember being completely amazed when I actually made this thing and it stood up in the studio and you could walk round it. I've made a sculpture! Finally I've

space

PHOTOGRAPH: ROBIN ALLISON SMITH PHOTOMONTAGE © 1998 ARUP ASSOCIATES, WOLF OLINS

managed to make something that isn't lying on the floor or leaning against a wall or hidden somewhere. It was about making something that was present – present in the world rather than excusing itself.

When you were talking about contemporary influences, you mentioned Nauman, Serra and Andre; but for old art, you named two painters rather than sculptors. If I had been asked to guess what art of the past your work was most related to, I'd have said Egyptian sculpture.

Funnily enough, I'm going to Egypt in two weeks' time. I've always wanted to go there, but have never been. I've spent many hours in the British Museum with Egyptian art. There's a piece I made called 'False Doors' that was actually very influenced by Egyptian work in some way. There were these two doors, six blocks of plaster which were very close to the wall, and you would only see the entrance of the doors from the other side of it. It was a very simple piece. It was about false entrances, I suppose – something that looked like absolutely nothing at all, but then you glanced round the side of it and could see this impression. I think there was a kind of Egyptian influence there. But generally not, actually. I recently did a Piero della Francesca tour in Italy and went to the Carrara quarries. What was so extraordinary about this place was the fact that you knew all these people had been there, Michelangelo and people. You could virtually see the evidence on these mountain ranges – the first part of the mountain range was flat where they had just taken off these massive lumps of marble, like with a cheese cutter. Actually that interests me more: the history of where that happened hundreds and hundreds of years ago; how these things went from A to B, massive lumps of stuff, and somehow ended up as the 'David'. I was really taken by this notion – I'm not quite sure why. I think the physics or the engineering of how these things were made – also with the Egyptians – is what fascinated me. The Mayans and all sorts of people made these extraordinary structures. It makes building projects like the Millennium Dome now look…

There's so much public sculpture that doesn't appear effortless; it looks like mammoth construction has gone on

Previous page and left: inverting space, time and matter – a computer simulation of Rachel Whiteread's Trafalgar Square plinth project. Facing page: subtle monumentalism – Whiteread's 'Water Tower' project above West Broadway and Grand Street, SoHo, New York, for the remainder of 1999. Pages 44/45: 'Untitled' (Book Corridors), 1997-1998

Your talking about this makes me perceive a relationship between your work and Stonehenge that, oddly enough, I had not thought about before.

I haven't been there for years but, as a kid, when you were allowed to run around it, I must have been three or four times and was certainly amazed by it.

The sense of the slab with no adornment is relevant.

Also, for instance, with the 'Book Corridors' piece. And when I first made 'Ghost' I remember someone saying it was like the Egyptian temple that's in the Metropolitan. In this sense it is, but it's not really, it's a room that's been put inside a room. When I made 'Ghost', I was interested in relocating a room, relocating a space from a small domestic house into a big public concrete anonymous place, which is what the museums have done over the world for years and years. It is always a pleasure for me to see this mass of stuff, which has taken months and months to make, finally sitting there with no one around, everything cleared away, walls white, as if it's just blown there. With things like the 'Water Tower' project that I have just done in New York, to make something look simple is the hardest thing in the world – to break it down so it's virtually not there. It was a nightmare to make it, and 'House' was a nightmare to make – these things that look effortless once they are just sitting there. I think it's about finding the right place for them as well. They have to be sitting in the right place. There's so much public sculpture that doesn't appear effortless; it looks like some mammoth construction has gone on, and it's all about the history of how it has got there rather than looking as if it's just flown there.

It's very interesting that the smaller bookcase piece is in some way close to painting, while the big one has nothing to do with painting at all.

I think my drawings are still very painterly and occasionally I'll make a painterly sculpture. I don't often use colour – it's generally the innate colour of the material. The smaller bookcase piece was almost accidental because I had made these other pieces and realised that the sci-fi and James Bond novels and things with coloured leaves would emboss on the surface of the work. So I decided to make a piece in colour. And just the way the plaster makes the colour bleed is like a watercolour. It's exactly the same process: you apply the plaster with the moisture, and you have to get it at exactly the right time, otherwise it doesn't work. It's really like sitting there doing a watercolour in bright sunlight. It goes all wrong immediately because it's too hot. I haven't said this to anybody before, but there's this very sad, dishevelled old library in Hackney that I go past virtually every day. It has a glass frontage with stands out of which these old ladies take their books. I hadn't realised until I was making the 'Book Corridors' piece that that was where the image had come from. So, there's a lot of real life in my work, I think.

And real death too.

And real death, lots of real death.

Your first bed piece was made very shortly after your father's death?

Yes, the very first piece, the plaster one. It's called 'Shallow Breath'.

I'd say that your work is often about redeeming decrepitude, or even redeeming death – the death of places as well as the death of people. Am I being over-romantic?

I think that you're not being over-romantic. That's definitely been in the work and is still in it. But as one develops as an artist, the language becomes the language of the pieces you have made previously, building up a thesaurus, really. A lot of my work is influenced by earlier work, as well as the decrepit libraries of Hackney or the junk shops or the people sleeping in the street, or whatever.

You've had a beautifully organic development so far.

I think a lot of that actually is to do with the fact that,

although I've been very pressured in many ways, I have tried to keep it to a minimum. I've been lucky to have had very few gallery shows and a lot of museum exhibitions, so I've had many opportunities to see a lot of work together and realise the path I was going through. There are also things like the Holocaust memorial. When I was asked to put in a proposal, I thought about it very hard, and the reason I agreed was that I had lived in Germany for a year and a half so I felt I wasn't going to a place that I didn't know about. But I went into this thing completely naively; not completely naively, but I didn't think for a moment that I would win it, I really didn't, and it was more about trying to see if I could make something. I was sort of challenging myself. Then I won it, which was quite a shock, and I've tried to make it happen since then. A lot of my work has been about challenges: challenging how I have made things previously and trying to push things in a way. Again, if you have a lot of commercial pressure, you don't necessarily have the freedom to do that. It depends how people work as artists, but my output is actually quite small and I hope to keep it that way, because I make or am involved with virtually every piece. I'm there from the beginning to the

end. I very rarely farm things out and that enables me to keep in touch with it. I think a lot of it is to do with having originally trained as a painter. The surface is absolutely 100 per cent the piece. And if I go to a foundry – I am working in one at the moment – the finish is not really being applied by the artist any more. It's more like putting a patina on something. It is a very traditional process and it looks like a bronze. But I have never been interested in doing that. I remember seeing some Cy Twombly sculptures years ago at the Whitechapel and being really taken with them because I thought they were bronzes that had been painted with white emulsion. I think they are absolutely beautiful, but I don't think they are what I thought they were. I think they are actually patinas. It looked like he had this work that the foundry had spent months and months making and he had just tossed on some white paint at the end of it. So it became something else; it became this almost throwaway gesture on top of this very complicated structure. Maybe it is about having trained as a painter…

It would be interesting to see whether you ever resume painting.

Well, a lot of the drawings are like paintings in that they involve colour. I did most of my drawing, I suppose, when I was living in Berlin. Most of them were about getting rid of the drawing: I used Tippex pens the whole time, which is probably a terrible thing to use in terms of stuff falling off the paper at some point. It was all about drawing a line, not being quite right, always using ink and then getting rid of the line with quite a fine white line, building things up in that way and then using a lot of watercolour on top. So they are very painterly drawings.

You were talking about colour in your sculpture and not messing about with the surfaces in the sense of putting on paint to colour them.

'A Hundred Spaces', probably the most colourful sculpture I ever made, was a series of 100 chair spaces, nine different chairs, three different types of resin and three different types of catalyst. By mixing and changing the catalyst I could change the colour without using any pigment. It was a very complicated thing to do. It is about a kind of purity, I suppose, in material. I know the colour's there and I can work with it. With plasters, I looked for dental plasters that were yellow and pink. And a lot of the rubbers I've used have been very like what I imagine the inside of your flesh to look like, very physical in that way. I said to one company I worked with: "What I want" (I think they thought I was completely mad) "is that in making this piece" (they were designing a rubber for me) "don't use any pigment, but just with the materials that you've got I want this to look like the first piss in the morning, I want it to be that colour." And they were like, "Oh, OK, we'll try that out." They made this fantastic colour – never been able to repeat it, but it was a good moment. And the piece was 'Mortuary Slab', in this colour, cast from a mortuary slab.

What do you feel about Brancusi?

Brancoosh.

Brancoosh indeed…

What do I feel about him? To be honest, not a great deal. I find him a bit sweet actually.

One might say there was a relationship between your

work and stone pieces of his such as 'The Kiss' and 'The Gate of the Kiss'.

I was going to say I don't really find them tough enough. I remember years ago seeing a Rückriem show, whom I'm not a great fan of at all, but enjoying the way these things were made and put together, or not made really: just decisions and drillings and breakages and putting back together of the form. I think it's to do with carving, actually. I think it's to do with inventing something, knowing that there was a block there, and then working a form out from within that block. Maybe that's just something to do with the traditions of sculpture and something that I was never interested in. I don't think I've ever carved anything. Maybe I did a bit of woodcarving at one point, but I certainly haven't done any stone carving.

Tell me more about carving or not carving.

I don't know that there's much more to say, really. If you look at someone like Andre, his early pieces made with wood are incredibly brutal and sort of carved. It seemed to be about making an immediate decision rather than something that you would fiddle around with for hours. It's about a process – of making a mark with a process, or breaking something at a certain point. I suppose the way I make my work, I am sort of carving. If I am making the space under a table, I'm actually carving space, and I decide where the edge of something is going to be and how it's going to be broken up, but it's all done in the negative, knowing that it's going to be filled with the material. I've never really thought about this before, actually. Does that make sense to you? If I'm looking at a mattress and make a decision where it is going to be cut in half, or where the edge of it is going to be, it's really, I suppose, making a decision that you would make if you had a block of something and you were carving it. But I'm doing it backwards.

In the negative.

So maybe I am a carver at heart?

There are basically three kinds of sculpture: carving, modelling and construction or assemblage. I would say your work was really a form of carving.

Yes. That had never ever occurred to me.

The three pieces in your new show which are like tombs, and also the 'Book Corridors', are, in concept, carvings, and they have the inner light of stone carving.

I had never thought about it before this moment – that it's carving. Especially with the book pieces. I hand-stacked every single stack of books myself and spent quite a long time doing it: if it wasn't quite right, I took them all out and started again.

And physically that is very much assemblage.

Yes, but it's all about knowing exactly what the plaster will do and what colour it will take from the book, what the undulations of the books are going to do. There are some other pieces I have made recently using hard-backed books and then ripping them out. It's an incredibly aggressive thing to do to destroy a lot of books. I always use second-hand ones, but I feel very bad about destroying them, and I always get them pulped afterwards so that they somehow go back into the world, rather than just chucking them in the skip. I have a conscience about it. But with these hard-backed books, you know, you put them in and then they're cast and then you're ripping them out and there is so much of the book actually left in it. Which is why I started to do this, because it leaves a sort of colour of the edge of the jacket and there are bits of paper still attached to it. But it's a really brutal way of making something. All of these things have come out though the frustration of the Holocaust memorial and I think that when that is made I will stop making book pieces. It's a frustration working in the studio miles away from Vienna while all these bureaucrats argue about it. It's my exorcism, being in the studio.

So your work is technically contrary to carving but conceptually a form of carving?

Mmm. This could change my life, this conversation. I'll get all these massive blocks of marble and start.

Well, you spoke with great passion about Carrara.

You know the last thing I want to do is go and order a lump of marble from Carrara. But it was an extraordinary place, absolutely extraordinary. It's white. The air is white and the sky is blue, but everything is white. There's this dust everywhere. And awful, awful sculptures all over the place. Absolutely dreadful. But you go off into the mountains and it's extraordinary. Just these trucks with these massive white lumps, as big as this room, on the back going down these tiny roads. And the way they take the marble out: when it's in the ground, it's very soft, almost like cheese, and they literally use these cables like cutting cheese. Marcus Taylor and I went into these places you weren't supposed to go, where they had signs that said "No Entry". We went inside these mountain sides which are like cathedrals of space, where they had taken out these lumps of marble, that go back maybe 200, 400, 500 metres, and there were these phenomenal caverns, just completely surrounded by marble. They were just beautiful. It's amazing taking stuff like that out of the earth in that way. There are all these ladders that have been left where you can climb up on to these ledges and walk inside them. It's a bit like in the south of England where they've quarried. Do you know a place called Dancing Ledge in Dorset? They've quarried Portland stone straight into the sea, basically. There are all these beautiful ledges you can walk along, and then they sometimes go to the hillside as well. They are like a man-made Giant's Causeway, but in an organised fashion, so it's all very rigid and angular.

I suddenly thought of scale as you were talking about landscape. Do you have problems deciding the size of the works? Of course, if you are doing a bath, a mattress, or a house, it's given.

Exactly. I don't think I have ever made anything that hasn't been related to my own physicality, my scale. I think that started originally in the studio when I was working on my own and occasionally got trapped underneath one of my sculptures. I remember getting my hand caught underneath something, being stuck there for two hours very late at night, trying to figure out how to release my hand without breaking it or wrecking the sculpture. It's definitely grown out of that very hands-on way of working. The 'Water Tower' in New York, despite being the biggest thing other than 'House' that I have produced as a single object (most of my works are in sections that stack together), retains that human scale. It is twelve feet high and nine feet wide and it really changes with the light. That was something I wanted when I was making it, but I didn't know if it would work. On a white day you can hardly see it at all, on a blue day it is very blue and like a jewel. At night it's like this smudge, you can just about pick it out. And when it's a full moon it lights the side of it. It's kind of fabulous what it does with light. I was there about three weeks ago and I thought it might have got dirty from the pollution, but it's sparkling. I think it has been raining quite a lot so it just gets cleaned. I was also expecting lots of birds to crap on it, but not a drop.

It was a kind of crazy moment when I was asked to do something over there very soon after 'House'. I'd had it with the street and the abuse that I got over 'House'. I'd spent a lot of time in New York but you just can't contend with New York at street level. I didn't want to try to make a sculpture in that chaos. I felt that it needed to be something that you didn't have to look at if you didn't want to. I was there recently and Tony Smith – do you like his work?

I like it very much. I've never been overwhelmed by it as I am by Serra or Judd or Nauman.

There was a piece outside the Seagram building that was fantastic. It was wonderful to see work like that on that scale. There was this fantastic building, then this yellow piece, then these yellow taxis everywhere – exactly the same yellow. Everything worked together. I'm trying to think of great examples of public sculpture; there are so few of them, but the ones that are great are architectural in some way and become part of the city rather than an ornament. You know there is an empty plinth on Trafalgar Square, and I was asked to put in a proposal for it. I thought why on earth do I want to do something in Trafalgar Square?

> **This could change my life, this conversation. I'll get all these massive blocks of marble and start...**

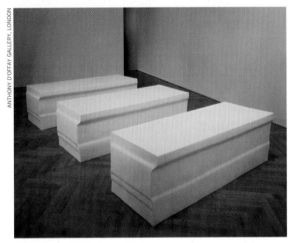

ANTHONY D'OFFAY GALLERY, LONDON

Then I went down there and spent a day looking at it, looking at the buildings and the people, the buses, Nelson's Column, just taking it all in and taking some photographs. It occurred to me that I didn't particularly want to put anything there, but there was something I could do which could work incredibly well – to cast the plinth in a transparent material like that used for the 'Water Tower' and invert it so it becomes a mirror of itself: you can see through it and it distorts the buildings. It's almost like making nothing... it's a beautiful object, this plinth, and it would become almost like a building and part of the square. I put in this proposal, which was accepted, but at the time I hadn't come across the problems that we encountered when I made the 'Water Tower'. It was technically very difficult to make. I'm sure we can overcome the technical problems, but at the moment I'm the only person with the knowledge of how to get this thing going, and what I would like to do is actually say: "Right, this is what we're going to do; you do it." Because all the processes involved in the mould-making become so removed from my own hand anyway that I think I could probably get someone else to do it. But the physical problems of the material are phenomenal, and it's whether or not we

Casting a new light on the art of carving. Above: 'Untitled' (Book Shelves), 1997-1998. Above left: 'Untitled' (Elongated Plinths), 1998

can do it. We shall see... When I realised 'House' was going to be on land with grass around it, I thought: fantastic, we'll have this wonderful open space and the ground will become like a plinth, elevating this object. Similarly with the 'Water Tower' – the house and the dunnage that it sits on is all part of the architecture of the street. It's not really so different from making something in an interior space. The Holocaust memorial is in quite a small square and the four or five entrances into it are almost like doorways into a room. If someone asked me to make something in a sculpture park, I'd say no. I don't work in that way. It has to be absolutely connected with the street, or connected to our environment. For me, it's not about taking something and putting it there. When I made 'House' there was a suggestion that it went to Milton Keynes, which was, for me, a completely barmy idea.

I think you said you didn't want to put it on wheels...
I often think about 'House', and I drive past the site regularly. I think if it were still there, it would look so sad, completely covered in graffiti, and I'm sure people would have destroyed it. People became so violent about it, whether they loved it or hated it. They wrote love poems on it; they were absolutely involved with this thing. And then it got all covered in paint. By the end, it looked a bit sad. If we'd been able to care for it, it might have been OK. What makes me really sad is that it never got a chance to become invisible. Every moment that it was up it had to fight for its life. It just didn't have a chance to sit there with any sort of dignity.

On the other hand, here was a piece of thoroughly contemporary art and the public seemed to appreciate it.
And still do, actually. I always think taxi drivers are a very good temperature gauge in society. If I tell them I'm an artist, they'll want to know what kind of stuff I do. Occasionally I say: "Well, you might have seen something I made years ago called 'House'." They go: "No, I don't know what you're talking about," and I say: "Do you ever drive down Grove Road, in the East End? Do you remember that great big concrete thing?" and they go: "You made *that*?" and they nearly crash the cab. Then they either say they loved it or hated it. One told me: "I remember picking someone up from Heathrow, and they said 'Take me to the House' and I just drove them all the way." It was amazing, the sense in the street. When it really kicked in, it was just chaos down there, hundreds and hundreds of people just milling around.

It did have a positive public impact and there may be a lesson there in what does.
I think one of the reasons my work is kind of popular is that it's connected with everybody's lives. People are threatened by modern art. They feel that they can't understand it, that they're not going to be able to understand it, and they immediately put up a barrier. Because so many of my pieces are connected with what everybody has in their homes or relates to in their daily lives, they make them think twice about something. 'House' made people think about the places they've lived in, and the walls they live in. Even though it was actually quite a large house, it was incredibly humble. Sort of sobering, I think.

Rachel Whiteread's project for the Trafalgar Square plinth will be on show in the year 2000. The Holocaust memorial in Vienna is due to be completed later this year

Concorde would have been good. Concorde would have been nice. More than that, Concorde would have been appropriate, and how often can you say that, those two words appearing together in the same sentence, and not even a "not" between them: Concorde, appropriate.

In December 1977, Chris Burden flew a model aeroplane, of balsa and tissue with a rubber band engine, down the central aisle of an Air France Concorde bound from Paris to Washington. As the artist has stated: "In accordance with Einstein's theories, the velocity of my model airplane as seen from the earth is the sum of the velocity of the Concorde (approx 1,400mph) plus the velocity of my model airplane (approx 10mph). My model airplane thus travelled faster than the supersonic Concorde." The plane was then placed within a small clear perspex box, complete with a laconic description of the performance. The work is called 'CBTV to Einstein', the surname referring both to the scientist and, coincidentally, the collectors who now own it. I recently included the plane in an exhibition, and here I am, crossing the Atlantic to meet the artist. And so Concorde would have been nice. Concorde would have been good. But Concorde doesn't fly to Los Angeles… ▶

Flying
in the face of art

In the early 1970s Chris Burden had himself shot at and nailed to a car in the name of art, but for the past two decades the influential American has moved away from performance and devoted himself to creating dramatic installations. While Burden was preparing an airplane factory for a London showing this spring, *tate* flew Jeremy Millar to southern California to find out more

Perhaps, given the performances which Burden has endured in his early career, spending 24 of the next 96 hours in a 767-300 is the least I can do.

We're sitting on the steps outside his studio, high in the hills of Topanga Canyon. It's bright and warm and we're surrounded by trees. The tape is punctuated by continuous dog barks and the sound of light aircraft overhead.

"The Tate asked me to do an exhibition, in the Duveen Galleries, and so I went to London, several times, and tried to come up with a proposal. I actually told them about my idea for an airplane factory, one of the things I had on the back burner that I wanted to do someday. I thought about it more and more and looked at the space... Part of the problem for me was how to deal with that odd, odd space. It's both a sort of public hall and... it's not traditionally what you'd think of as a gallery in the sense of a nice white room with two doors at either end. It's an odd space

This airplane factory is going to be a tinkerer's wet dream, so to speak...

because the architecture is so dominant too, such a long awkward space. I kept looking at it and thinking about it and I proposed building this real factory that would make these stick and tissue rubber-band-powered airplanes that I've used a lot in my works. The focus would be to use the central rotunda, basically, as the focal point, and the machinery for the factory could be in one of the corridors, and the planes could be launched and fly in the central rotunda and fly back down; apparently, there's an alarm up there I'm not supposed to go by or something because the fire brigade comes out and there's a £700 fine, but maybe that's one of my goals..."

"They shouldn't have told you that..."

"No. But if I could make this spectacular machine and have it launch these planes, I wouldn't have to deal with the rest of the space – really it's an architectural/sculptural problem in a certain sense: how do you make something in that space? My solution was to ignore most of it and to concentrate on this one central area."

"It energises the rest of the space then..."

"Yeah..."

"Because the empty space becomes a material that you're working within."

"And part will be the machinery – it won't take up that much space, really. It wasn't just the flat ground space, it was also the volume. I thought about the Erector Set [Meccano] bridges and stuff like that but... ach... it was something about taking command of this volume too, and somehow this plane spiralling round in there and coming back down occupies the space in a certain sense and takes

control of it, makes use of that wonderful volume, and celebrates it."

Of course, the effect that a bridge has on the surrounding space is well known – didn't Heidegger say that a bridge gathers the landscape around it? – and it is an effect which is difficult to ignore here, in this city of freeways and flyovers. (And, of course, we shouldn't forget Duchamp's quip about American art: plumbing and bridges.) The Erector Set bridges are being made in the studio behind us, thousands of metal strips, nuts, bolts; one is complete, based on a drawing in a book for a bridge which was never built. It has high, thin arches and could be walked under with ease. Another, about twenty feet long and based on a railway bridge on the Upper West side of Manhattan, is still under construction and lies on its side. Another is about the size of a foot stool, a demonstration model, a model of a model, yet it easily supports Burden. "The arch is working." But it wouldn't have worked in the Duveen Galleries; Burden thought the airplane factory a more appropriate choice.

"England gave birth to the industrial age, it was the first country to industrialise, and it may also be the first to have got bored with it. Its industry has declined, and I'm sure there are many reasons for that, but there does seem to be a spiritual rejection on some level, a lack of interest. I know from my own interests that England is a country of hobbyists and tinkerers, and they're good at it, inventors, y'know. There is this great fascination with machinery, but it's on an individual level, not on a corporate level. That's why I thought that the airplane factory would be good for England because this factory is going to be a tinkerer's wet dream, so to speak..."

In 1970, the German-born, British-based economist E F Schumacher published an essay called "Peace and Permanence" in *Resurgence, Journal of the Fourth World*. In it he asked: "What is it that we really require from the scientists and technologists? I should answer: We need methods and equipment which are:
" – cheap enough so that they are accessible to virtually everyone;
" – suitable for small-scale application; and
" – compatible with man's need for creativity."

These are sentiments which Burden almost certainly shares. Between August and October 1975, Burden "conceived, designed and constructed a small, one-passenger automobile. My goal was to design a fully operational four-wheeled vehicle which would travel 100 miles per hour and achieve 100 miles per gallon. I conceived of this vehicle as extremely light weight, streamlined and similar in structure to both a bicycle and an airplane." Although the car was exhibited in the Galerie Stadler in Paris, the 'B-Car' was less a "relic" from a previous performance, as his many other objects had been, than the outcome of a complex struggle between theory

and its practical application (and as Schumacher later writes: "An ounce of practice is generally worth more than a ton of theory"). A couple of years later, for "documenta 6" in Kassel, Burden made 'CBTV' (Chris Burden Television), a complete working demonstration of John Logie Baird's primitive mechanical television. Both pieces play an extremely important role in Burden's relationship to technology.

"It's about trying to gain some control or mastery in the world. The two big technological projects, for me, were the 'B-Car' and the television system ('CBTV') – two big consumer projects. The fact that I made them, like Robinson Crusoe, gave me a tremendous thrill, just personally, because it's like 'Oh my God, I don't have to buy a GM car, do I?' Baird inventing TV with a mechanical pie disk inspired me to make one, I mean, a revolving pie disk! 'Let's go down the supermarket and get a pie disk and make a TV!' It's very subversive in a certain sense because the last thing this capitalist system wants is everyone to be home knitting."

As he noted in the original statement which accompanied 'CBTV': "As technology becomes more and more complex, fewer and fewer people have any understanding of how anything really works." It is this mystification which Burden attempts to disperse. In creating pieces which are visually intelligible, he encourages the viewer to understand, by themselves, for themselves, the technological or scientific processes which they are witnessing. It is a belief which continues in 'When Robots Rule: The Two Minute Airplane Factory'. The complete process, from the loading of materials into the "factory" to the flight of the finished product two minutes later, will be made visible to the gallery visitor. Even if it breaks down, even if the visitor can't see it working, he or she should be able to see what isn't working; and so the process continues.

In fact, that isn't the whole process; the visitor is implicated further. As each plane lands following its maiden flight, it will be retrieved by a gallery attendant, who will then take it to the gallery shop, nearby, where it will be available for purchase at a very low cost: "The experience is watching the product be made and being able to purchase it also. It is not a model of a factory, but a real one." In becoming a consumer of the work, the visitor also takes on certain responsibilities: will the work be flown or will it be kept in a box? "My vision is that these schoolchildren buy them and take them out and immediately try to fly them on the steps of the Tate. They go off at

The last thing this capitalist system wants is everyone to be home knitting

This airplane has most threequarters of
hours of flight time, and only needs
to be recovered in order to fly again

AIRPLANE and BARBED WIRE

**Winging it. Opening spread: 'The Two
Minute Airplane Factory', 1998. Above:
'Airplane and Barbed Wire', 1979**

awkward angles and very few are retrieved
for a second flight. A lot of them will end
up smash 'n' crash in the immediate vicinity,
like a Barry Le Va scatter piece...."

In this simple act of placing the planes on
sale, Burden raises a number of important
issues with regard to the visitor/consumer.
The issues with regard to the gallery itself are
more complex yet. "The real question is: will
we be able to sell enough of these things? If
we end up with a surplus of 200 planes a day,
what do we do? We'll have a thousand planes
left over in the first five days – what do we
do with them? Store them? Send them to
children's homes? I don't know. A lot of these
things need to be worked out and some will
only be worked out while we're actually in the
process... It might not be a problem. We
might sell surplus stock on busier days. But
it does take on this other dimension, not just
a model of a factory, of industrialisation,
but actually a factory; not just a model of
capitalism, of consumerism, but actually those
things." And these are things which need
urgent exploration: "The West is based on
this idea of eternal growth: more, more, more.
Not as much as last year, always more. Wait
a minute, how can that be? At some point
there's gonna be a day of reckoning,
something's gonna pop.

"I teach at UCLA and there's all this
money thrown around for new digital
equipment. So, I've been trying to conceive
of a class called Luddite 101, and the lab fee

buys you a sledgehammer: 'Go to it – the
first assignment is to find the highest priced
piece of electronic equipment and smash it to
smithereens. After you've completed your first
assignment, come back and I will direct you to
further intrusions into the electronic world.' "

From the very beginning of his career,
Burden has questioned the experiences and
ideas which we take for granted, whether
through the endurances of his early
performances or the elegance of his
technological demonstrations. In laying bare
these structures, he is attempting to
reintroduce us to the fundamentals of
production, and that means the acquisition
of mental skills as much as technical ones.
It is romantic, certainly, but also insistently
pragmatic; indeed, Burden has managed to
make the pragmatic a romantic position.
Perhaps it is because of this relentless
questioning that it is difficult to place Burden,
or his work, politically. His belief in forms
of intermediate technology would no doubt
have met the approval of Schumacher, as
mentioned earlier; and the 'B-Car' could
almost have been advertised in the *Whole
Earth Catalog*, the community-based,
environmentally conscious publication
established by Stewart Brand in 1968. It was
these values, which we might broadly associate
with the Left, that were being consolidated on
the American west coast while Burden was a
student; and yet, at the same time, isn't this
hand-made, hands-off self-sufficiency also
reminiscent of the extreme Right survivalist
groups which seem to litter America's
wilderness? Wasn't the first line of the

My vision is that children buy them and try to fly them on the steps of the Tate

Unabomber's Manifesto, "The Industrial
Revolution and its consequences have been
a disaster for the human race"? Perhaps what
is most important about Burden's project,
therefore, is that he reminds us of the
uncertainties of any genuinely critical position.
It is not simply a taking of sides, an
unthinking defence of a "yes", or a "no", but
an ongoing engagement, a continuous process
of questioning. He reminds us that the
exploration of a subject is not the same as its
condonation, and that the position of criticism
is one of fascinated, often appalled, curiosity.

I'm back in London. I take a break from
typing and go to get the papers. Walking back
down the street, I read that a government
agency is advising people to stockpile two
weeks' worth of food for the new year, 2000,
should the millennium bug affect distribution
services. I think about Chris Burden – I had
just listened to some of his comments about
the bug on tape – and wonder how it would
affect him. I'm not sure it would, not directly,
not up at his house in Topanga. No, he's
already prepared. He'll be just fine.
*Chris Burden, 'When Robots Rule: The
Two Minute Airplane Factory', sponsored
by American Airlines, Tate Gallery, London,
2 March-13 June. Jeremy Millar flew to
Los Angeles courtesy of American Airlines*

worker
The
aesthetic

Artists used to yearn to be gentlemen, argues James Hall, but the past 150 years has seen the rise of the cult of the artist worker

During nearly a decade spent visiting innumerable art galleries as a full-time critic, I have been repeatedly struck – literally as well as metaphorically – by the way that modern artworks (paintings as well as sculptures) address the viewer. I keep seeing things that pull away, and jut out, from walls; that loom up directly from the floor, swoop down from ceilings and slice through walls. And how many times have I been surrounded, squeezed, trapped, blocked and tripped? At the last Turner Prize exhibition, for example, I stepped warily round a floor-hugging, booby-trapped zip of a sculpture by Cathy de Monchaux, as furry as it was fanged; and I recoiled from Chris Ofili's customised, off-road paintings, bejewelled and bull-barred in elephant dung.

I have been no less impressed by the very different body of language of earlier art. Whereas modern works have few qualms about invading the viewer's own space, old master sculpture and painting prefers to occupy a more distinct realm. Paintings usually consist of flat, seamless expanses of oil and canvas, neatly cordoned off by a frame, while statues tend to be made with a framing wall, niche or pedestal in mind.

There has clearly been a seismic shift in ways of seeing. From the Renaissance until the nineteenth century, the ideal maker and viewer of

Art for hedonism's sake. Michelangelo Buonarroti, 'The Drunkenness of Bacchus', 1496-1497, and detail of the satyr (left)

an artwork was assumed to be stationary and/or sedentary; since then, the ideal maker and viewer is increasingly imagined to be restless and on the move. We have to look at modern paintings not just from the front, but from the sides and all sorts of oblique angles, while modern sculptures can be walked around, into, over and under. But how do we account for the change in emphasis from flattish images to multi-faceted objects? One of the most revealing ways to explain it is by looking at developments in the image of the artist. To put it crudely: whereas artists in the Renaissance yearned to be gentlemen, modern artists yearn to be workers. Gentlemen don't tend to move around that much, peer round corners or bend over, but workers do.

From the fifteenth century, artists in Italy were keen to improve their status and no longer be seen as artisans who were subject to the rules of a guild, as had been the case in the Middle Ages. To

do this, they played down the manual aspects of their trade – and emphasised the conceptual and contemplative aspects. Yet as soon as they tried to distinguish themselves from manual workers, a new fissure opened up between painters and sculptors. For some painters and their apologists, sculptors were a hindrance to their own social and intellectual ambitions – and they were also rivals for commissions. The pro-painting lobby claimed that the art of sculpture was more labour-intensive, and less sophisticated and versatile than painting: its practitioners were dirty beefcakes who lacked class. Such was the force of their arguments that painting came to determine the way in which people looked at sculpture.

Neighbours from hell

The most celebrated recipe for the gentleman artist was provided by Leonardo da Vinci in his *Notebooks*. He begins by caricaturing sculptors: "Sculpture is not a science but a very mechanical art because it causes its executant sweat and bodily fatigue… His face becomes plastered and powdered all over with marble dust which makes him look like a baker, and he becomes covered in minute chips of marble, which makes him look as if he is covered in snow. His house is in a mess and covered in chips and dust from the stone." For Leonardo, a sculptor would be a neighbour from hell. He flails and flounders, scarcely able to see what he is doing. He is the lord and slave of confusion. Something along these lines is illustrated in an anonymous woodcut of 1527. It purports to show Michelangelo in action. He is a hot and bothered wild man, clad only in a loin cloth, about to crash his chisel into the chest of a work in progress – a reclining female nude lying on the ground. The sculptor squats over her, his knee digging into her groin. From the sculpture's alarmed facial expression, we infer that even she flinches at her maker's over-emphatic, seemingly murderous touch.

By and large, the Renaissance tried to avoid such uncontrolled and physical engagements with artworks. The mind had to be exercised, but not the body. Michelangelo would have frowned on this representation of himself as a Neanderthal, and virtually every other contemporary image of him shows him wrapped in elevated thoughts rather than marble chips. Such sober images conform to the account of the ideal artist which follows Leonardo's caricature of the sculptor. Here, Leonardo describes a well-dressed and urbane easel painter, who can listen to music or chat to authors while he works in a pleasantly furnished room, unhindered by the "crashing of hammers and other confused noises".

Most Renaissance sculptures demand a "rational" mode of apprehension: they are, in a literal as well as metaphorical sense, niche products. Only one of Michelangelo's works was designed to be circumnavigated, and all of his other surviving statues were meant to be placed against walls and in niches – or on tombs. 'David' was intended to be placed high up on the side of Florence Cathedral, hence its odd proportions. The viewer of Renaissance sculpture was expected to keep fairly still. This is epitomised by the so-called "Medusa topos", the highest form of praise for a statue. The conceit had it that viewers of a fine sculpture were more marble-like than the statue because they were rooted to the spot in amazement. In a poem written on Michelangelo's death in 1564, Laura Battifera degli Ammanati said that he "overwhelmed whoever saw his works and left them as if petrified".

The work that most invited circumnavigation was of the more exuberant, Dionysian kind, made for fountains and gardens. In other words, circumnavigation was associated with the primitive and the irrational. The first Renaissance sculpture that is generally credited with being planned fully in the round, rather than in relation to a series of fixed viewpoints, is Andrea del Verrocchio's 'Putto with a Dolphin' (early 1480s), which surmounted a fountain in the gardens of the Medici villa at Careggi. A podgy little boy grasps a dolphin. It is a slippery subject for a slippery viewing experience.

A well-rounded art

Michelangelo's only surviving work that was made to be walked around is, not surprisingly, his raunchiest. 'Bacchus' (1496-1497) was created for the garden of his Roman patron, Cardinal Raffaelo Riario, vice-chancellor of the papal court, but Riario probably found it too licentious because it soon entered another collection. It certainly is a disconcerting work. The God of Wine is completely naked, bar a cap made from bunches of grapes. He holds a cup, and seems to stagger backwards. Standing diagonally behind him is a satyr, who steals his grapes. The viewer of 'Bacchus', by having to circumnavigate, would be encouraged to feel a suitable state of inebriation. Michelangelo's biographer Condivi explained it as an allegory of the effects of strong drink.

But some viewers were inclined to view even fountain statues from fixed viewpoints. Benvenuto Cellini recounts how Duke Cosimo I came to see his model for the 'Neptune Fountain', and "he walked round it, stopping to inspect it from all four sides just as an expert would have done". Elsewhere, Cellini claimed that sculpture was superior to painting because it offered more views of the same subject. But the cultural fixer Vincenzo Borhini, who made some swingeing remarks about sculpture in general, and about Cellini in particular (he dismissed his protestations in favour of sculpture as the mere barkings of a butcher's mongrel), countered with a clever riposte: seeing a sculpture from different sides was just like seeing a succession of paintings. Thus, ways of seeing as derived from painting came to dominate. Stillness and tranquillity, both in the artist and the viewer, was grace. These notions (or prejudices) remained pretty much in force until the nineteenth century.

The ideal of the gentleman artist peaks during the nineteenth century, when it is challenged by a cult of the worker artist. This cult was to

Contemplating a new role for the artist. Auguste Rodin, 'The Thinker', 1880

change the course of art. Since sculptors already, by and large, had the status of workmen, the practice of sculpture gained a certain cachet. Thus we find, in the past 150 years, enormous numbers of painters trying their hand at sculpture. Not all of them would have thought of themselves as worker-artists, but many painters were drawn to sculpture by the myth of the workmanlike. The painter-sculptors range from academic artists such as Leighton and Gèrome, to the more avant-garde figures of Degas, Gauguin, Matisse and Miró. In the post-war period, Pollock, de Kooning, Fontana and Schnabel have all made sculpture. In addition, there are many painters who have made object-based art, such as Duchamp and Dalí. A German critic, writing in 1922, said that for many painters sculpture was a "secret love".

Directly related to this is a marked emphasis on the painting's status as an object: thick and complex impastoes, collage and shaped canvases have become ubiquitous. Some painter-sculptors were just momentarily slumming it, or flexing their creative muscles, but for a significant majority, object-based art has answered a genuine need. It allows painters to imagine that their art partakes of, and projects into, the "real" world: it no longer hangs aloofly on a wall.

Gustave Courbet (1819-1877) is the first important example of a worker-artist. Symptomatically, he is a painter who used thick impastoes, and who made sculpture. In an early self-portrait he presents himself as a foppish sculptor in a wooded landscape, carving into natural rock. His career as a sculptor really got underway in 1861, when he opened an art school in Paris. Instead of dictating to his students, he proposed to run it as a "group atelier, recalling the fruitful collaborations of the Renaissance ateliers". The first piece that Courbet made was a statue for the centre of a fountain, 'Boy Catching Bullheads'. And his revolutionary painting technique, using a palette knife, spatula and his fingers, and adding sand to his oil paint, could also be seen in sculptural terms. Caricaturists sometimes represented his pictures as bas-reliefs.

By the second decade of the twentieth century, the cult of the worker-artist was so deeply entrenched that artists felt able to take the notion to unimagined extremes. During the development of Cubism, Picasso and Braque regularly wore blue mechanics' outfits. Their dealer Daniel Kahnweiler recalled them arriving at the gallery one day "cap in hand acting like labourers". They immediately announced: "Boss, we're here for our pay." But it was more than a matter of costume and demeanour. They worked together as "collaborators" until their paintings became almost indistinguishable, and they even gave up signing their work on the front of the canvas: sometimes they got Boischaud, Kahnweiler's assistant, to sign for them on the back. The only form of writing that appeared on the front of the canvas was stencilled letters of newsprint. Picasso explained: "We felt the temptation, the hope of an anonymous art, not in its expression, but in its point of departure." In 1952, while recalling the achievements of Cubism, he told Kahnweiler: "But one cannot do it alone, one must be with others... It requires teamwork." This may have been the reason why Apollinaire claimed in *The Cubist Painters* (1912) that Courbet was "the father of the new painters". It wasn't too long before their art started to take a three-dimensional turn. Braque was probably experimenting with paper sculpture in the summer of 1911, for in September of that year he wrote to Kahnweiler saying how much he missed "the collaboration of Boischaud in making my painted papers". The following year he added sand and metal filings to his paint and simulated the appearance of wood grain and marbling with a house decorator's comb. Braque knew about these techniques because he came from a family of house decorators. In September 1912, he glued wood grain wallpaper to the canvas, thus making his first *papiers collés*.

Cubed roots

At the time that Braque was making the paper sculptures, he had signed a letter to Kahnweiler "Wilburg Braque". This nickname (after the American aviator Wilbur Wright) seems to have originated in 1908, when a review of his first Cubist paintings was placed above a news item about Wright's victory in an aviation contest. Picasso and Braque often went to see planes take off and land, and are reputed to have tried to make a model aeroplane. The frequent use of the name in 1912, however, is probably because Braque's sculptures had an angularity, fragility and home-made quality that reminded Picasso of Wright's biplanes. Wright's personality would also have been an attraction. He was portrayed by the leading aeronautical journalist in France as a simple man who had astonished the employees at the Bollee car factory (where the Flyer had been assembled) by his dedication and craftsmanship. A postcard shows him sewing a new patch of canvas on to the wing of his plane with a home-made needle.

Picasso used dressmakers' pins to experiment with the placement of cut paper and, on at least thirteen occasions, he left the pins in position in the completed work. This technique has been put down to his repeated exposure to women who practised dressmaking, but Wright's bouts of sewing and patching may also have been influential. No

Cubist collaborators (from right, clockwise). Pablo Picasso, 'Man with a Pipe', 1914; Picasso on the Cote d'Azur, 1957; Georges Braque, 'Still Life (JS Bach)', 1912; Portrait of Braque, Paris, 1949

wonder the art critic André Salmon, writing about Picasso and Braque in his book *La Jeune Sculpture Française* (1919), warned his readers not to underestimate their interest in "the beauty of artisanal work".

The Cubists' down-to-earth approach to art making was further emphasised by the fact that the canvases in their studios were casually laid on the floor, or placed on chairs and other pieces of furniture. There was no ideal viewing position for these pictures. Their constructions and collages also required an "engaged" viewer who was prepared to peer at their creases and into their crevices. Thus, the cult of the worker-artist made new demands on the viewer as well as on the artist.

Where sculpture in traditional media was concerned, a "workman-like" approach was bound up with its being both accessible and viewable from all sides. For this to happen, it had to assert its independence from architecture. An important catalyst was the display of the Elgin Marbles in the British Museum. Whereas in the Parthenon they had been placed high up, in London they were now at eye level. In 1818 the French sculptor-cum-connoisseur Quatremère De Quincy, in a series of formal "letters" on the Elgin Marbles addressed to leading neo-classical sculptor Antonio Canova, explained that whenever sculpture is integrated into architecture it loses its grandeur and specificity, for the viewer is compelled to take in the whole building (this was the traditional, "pictorial" treatment of sculpture). But in the British Museum the viewer is "on the building-site or in the studio itself, and the objects are to hand in their actual dimensions: you can move around each one, counting up the fragments, assessing relationships and measurements". Here, walking round a sculpture is not a disorientating, inebriating experience – as it had so often seemed to be in the Renaissance. Rather, it is a supremely logical and controlled act. The building-site/studio situation was to become the ideal.

The most important critic of sculpture of the late nineteenth century, Adolf von Hildebrand, regarded the divorce of sculpture from architecture as further evidence of democratic dumbing-down. In *The Problem of Form* (1893), he railed against the Victorian predilection for putting statues in the centre of public spaces: "Today the relief form of art scarcely exists. Sculpture to the modern man signifies some figure in the round, destined to stand in the centre of a public square." This kind of work, he believed, scarcely ranked higher than "convict labour". Figures were frequently placed at the base of monuments, and this meant that "no definite line" was drawn between the monument and the public; "we might as well bring a few stone spectators on the scene!"

Artist as thinker

The most successful nineteenth-century incarnation of all that Hildebrand abhorred is Auguste Rodin. With the possible exception of Picasso, no modern artist has been so celebrated and honoured. He was also the first sculptor working outside Italy to have a major international reputation. Central to the Rodin myth – and to his popularity – was the idea that he combined the down-to-earth practical skills of a *practicien* (a studio hand) with the lofty inspiration of a genius. He became a symbol of the artist in a modern democracy – even though many of his views were feudal rather than democratic. It was during and after the inauguration of 'The Thinker', placed in front of the Pantheon on a low pedestal in 1906, that the worker theme reached its apogee. It was seen as a self-portrait, representing a "thinker to the common soul" who does not forget that "it was he, bent to the earth, who first seeded and harvested". A writer in 1904 had claimed that either 'The Thinker' was Rodin's *practicien*, or that Rodin himself was a worker and that the sculpture "is a worker dreaming of his meagre salary, or of the difficulties of life". The bent figure of the sculptor, and the activities in his studio, had become a magisterial yet down-to-earth symbol of his age.

The cult of the worker-artist is in part a psychological defence mechanism against the isolation of the modern artist. It is an attempt to normalise the avant-garde. The more incomprehensible and distasteful modern art became to the art establishment and to the general public, the more artists protested their ordinary-Joe-ness and their connection with the "real" world. Leo Steinberg has written that to be workman-

Flushed with success. Right: Andy Warhol in his studio in New York, 1964. Facing page, top: Sarah Lucas with her 1996 sculpture 'The Great Flood'. Facing page, below: Claes Oldenburg and Coosje van Bruggen

© EVE ARNOLD/MAGNUM

like "is an absolute good. Efficiency is self-justifying: it exonerates any activity whatsoever... those activities which, like bloodshed and art, sometimes seem dubious on moral grounds – they more than any need the higher ideal of efficiency to shelter under." The avant-garde has been defined by the formation of groups and movements, some with their own manifestos. Creating a community, literal or imaginary, is a crucial part of being a modern artist. Most recently – and perhaps opportunistically – we have had the sculptors Christo and Claes Oldenburg crediting their wives as co-authors of their work.

Collaboration is thus central to the myth of the worker-artist. Duchamp stressed that the creative act is not performed by the artist alone. It is a collaborative act between the artist and the spectator. The spectator's act of interpretation "completed" the work. Sometimes he imagined the spectator to be a devoted aficionado, but at others he defined the spectator as "the whole of posterity and all those who look at works of art who, by their vote, decide that a thing should survive".

Collaboration not only takes place with people, real or imagined. It also takes place with materials. In 1948, Picasso looked back to 1912: "We sought to expressly relate with materials we did not know how to handle... we surrendered ourselves to [the work] completely, body and soul." One can extrapolate from this and see why object-based art has been so enticing to modern painters. It is an activity where, because they are not properly trained, they are not in complete control. To a certain extent they have to surrender to the materials. The materials, by default, are co-workers, with an equal say in the final appearance of the object. Related to this is Duchamp's famous description of the readymade as "a sort of rendezvous". The selection and discovery of the object is not a punitive or aggressive act on the part of the patriarchal artist. It is a formalised engagement between two consenting parties.

Material collaboration

There was much talk between the First and Second World Wars of sculptors who used direct carving techniques "collaborating" with stone or wood – instead of, as had previously been the case, collaborating with *practiciens*. In *Meaning of Modern Sculpture* (1932), the British critic R H Wilenski stated that modern sculptors regard direct carving "as a kind of collaboration between the sculptor and the substance". Something similar underpins Louise Bourgeois's decision to start working in marble instead of wood in 1967. In an interview with the sculptor Alain Kirili she explained that wood is "too soft a material" and "offers no resistance". When Kirili said that the resistance of the material is the "extraordinary advantage" of sculpture over painting, Bourgeois simply replied: "Painting doesn't exist for me."

The most celebrated post-war collaboration between men and materials is the one involving Robert Rauschenberg and Jasper Johns from the mid-1950s to the early 1960s. It, too, resulted in a dissatisfaction with painting and a migration into object-based art. Both artists had studios in the same building, and they were lovers for more than six years, until 1961. During this period Rauschenberg developed his mixed-media "combines" while Johns developed complex impastoes, sometimes incorporated objects into his painting, and from 1958-1961 made most of his sculptures (ale cans, flashlights, light-bulbs, paint brushes, etc). Rauschenberg saw his art as a collaboration with the real world: "I've always felt as though, whatever I've used and whatever I've done, the method was always closer to a collaboration with materials than any kind of conscious manipulation and control." His working method was another kind of rendezvous – and Johns was one of those "materials" with which he collaborated.

The ultimate manifestation of the worker-artist ethos is the construction of art galleries and museums in former factories and industrial buildings. The Tate Gallery of Modern Art in Bankside Power Station will be the apogee of this trend, though one might equally cite the Saatchi Gallery housed in a former paint factory. This phenomenon began with artists moving into lofts in former industrial districts after the war. A major attraction was that they were cheap and light, and spacious enough to accommodate large works, but the romantic associations of industrial and artisanal work were important too. A workshop

environment by no means always inspires object-based art, but it has certainly stimulated artists to think in such terms. When Andy Warhol moved into his so-called Factory on East 47th Street in November 1963 (it was a single 100x40ft room on the fifth floor of a former hat factory) his thoughts immediately turned to sculpture. His first new project was to make around 400 sculptures of grocery boxes for Campbell's tomato juice, Kellogg's Cornflakes, Del Monte peach halves, Brillo Pads, etc, out of plywood. The logos were silk-screened on to the boxes, which were nailed shut. Warhol worked on these sculptures for three months with his assistant Gerard Malanga. One observer said it looked like "a production line in a surrealist sweat-shop". Malanga subsequently said that this was the hardest he ever worked with Warhol.

The British artist Sarah Lucas is a typical recent incarnation of the worker-artist. In 1993, she collaborated with Tracey Emin on 'The Shop', an emporium established for six months in a shop front in London's East End. They sold merchandise such as Damien Hirst ashtrays and bits of bric-a-brac made on site. In the following year Lucas explained: "My work is about one person doing what they can. I like the hand-made aspect... I'm not keen to refine it. I enjoy the crappy bits around the back." So here we have it in a nutshell – an artist who inhabits a world with a back as well as a front proclaiming the utter ordinariness of what she does.

William Hogarth is usually hailed as the native-born father of British painting. Not so, says Waldemar Januszczak, it was William Dobson one hundred years earlier

The first great British painter?

William Dobson. Savour this name. In a moment, I will begin listing and discussing the many under-valued accomplishments of its obscure owner. But for the moment I want only to repeat it as Wagner repeated his new chord – as a tone setter, a starting sound. William Dobson. Does it not have an impressively plangent native ring? Is not its Englishness thoroughly unimpeachable?

Another of the unimpeachably English Williams – Hogarth – was recently the subject of much national adulation. The year 1997 marked Hogarth's 300th birthday. He was fêted as a portraitist, a satirist, the inventor of the painted novel, an energetic print-maker, etc. No one begrudges him this attention. His successes were real and multivalent. But behind the relentless Hogarth tercentenary celebrations, when so many exhibitions, at so many venues, dealt with so many different aspects of his achievements, there lay a widespread and casual assumption. And this assumption, which drove museums up and down the land to make their notable national fuss about Hogarth, certainly is challengeable. I am referring to the view that he was the first native artist of distinction.

It is something that children learn with their milk: British art found a voice of its own, at last, with Hogarth. The claim has been made so often that most people believe it. But it is not true. A hundred years earlier, a native artist, English born and bred, had a career that was considerably more remarkable than Hogarth's; but considerably shorter.

Surrounded by successful foreigners, this brilliant native found a way to paint unmistakably British pictures, a few of which were as inventive as anything being produced anywhere else in Europe at the time. He was preternaturally aware of Caravaggio. He studied Titian and Veronese. He had quick and fluent hands, and an obviously interesting psychology. He played a crucial part in a truly dramatic era in British political history. And, to cap it all, he undoubtedly invented that bluntness and directness of portraiture that is usually held to have been Hogarth's creation. William Dobson was the first native painter not only of distinction but also, in touches, of genius. As a foreigner myself, I can see this very clearly. What is beyond my ken is why the British can't see it for themselves.

Playing the national game of who came first is hardly ever useful. I would not be playing it here were it not for the fact that the stakes are so high. British art is poised on the threshold of a presentational revolution. The countdown to the splitting asunder of the Tate Gallery is now advanced. The modern collection has grabbed most of the resulting attention, and the creation of a new museum for twentieth-

PHILIP MOULD, HISTORICAL PORTRAITS LTD/BRIDGEMAN ART LIBRARY

Taking a new direction. Left: portrait of a man thought to be the artist, c.1640. Right: 'Portrait of John, 1st Lord Byron', c.1643

century art at the converted power station at Bankside is seen, quite rightly, as an event of immense national significance.

But where does this leave the Millbank Tate, the current building, charged with the task of celebrating and illuminating the tradition of British art? Bankside appears so stridently new that the Millbank Tate, with its traditional task, its classical portico, its Portland stone cladding, can hardly help but seem, in comparison, to be set in the past.

But the curious marvel of it is that the British collection at Millbank has far more to play for. There are many museums of contemporary art around the world. But there

can be only one national collection of British art. The crucial museum business of defining this collection, selecting its direction, deciding upon its emphasis, lies ahead. And it is here, in the struggle for a real national understanding of Britain's art past, that the tragedy of William Dobson deserves far more attention than it will receive.

Dobson was born in 1611. He died in 1646. That is not much of a life. He died a pauper, with a reputation for wildness, and was buried in St Martin in the Fields, bang opposite the current National Gallery, where, incidentally, there are no Dobsons on display, although there are, of course, numerous examples of

works by foreign artists in his milieu, by Van Dyck, in particular, and Rubens.

Dobson was said to have been Van Dyck's pupil, and then his successor as Charles I's court painter. But there are no official records left of any such appointment. Little survives of his times on paper. There are only three documents with Dobson's name on them. The first records his birth, the third records his death, and the one in between deals with guild business at the Painter-Stainers Company. The facts in his life are scarce. His pictures are rare, and scattered. It has been easy to overlook him.

So I do not know if you have heard of

Dobson before. But I do know that you certainly should have done. If we put together the few biographical facts that survive with the rare but resonant examples of his art, we can see immediately that he had one of the most telling of all British art careers. He found himself in the crossfire of one of the most significant moments of British domestic history, and to a remarkable extent he found himself embodying that moment. Those familiar with his work will probably know him as the pre-eminent portrayer of the English civil war, the chief portraitist of the doomed royalists. When Charles I took on Cromwell, it fell to Dobson to be at the king's side. So

Dobson's cavaliers are a familiar enough presence in history text-books and the like. Dashing in their scarlet sashes, intense and heroic, with cascades of romantic hair framing their doomed visages, these handsome losers were his best-known gift to posterity. And before we move on to his other achievements we should definitely stop to admire them.

I am going to quote you some lines of poetry. They will evoke the fabulous cut of Dobson's sitters far more eloquently than anything I can write. They come from a poem by the cavalier Robert Lovelace, whose portrait, half-heartedly ascribed to Dobson, hangs in the Dulwich Picture Gallery: long haired, gaunt, with a pencil-thin moustache and a sash over a suit of armour. Lovelace, poet/warrior/paramour/prisoner, was in love with Lucrasta, to whom he devoted a famous collection of heartbreakingly romantic verses, written in the London jail to which he had been sent after being captured by roundheads while leading a troop loyal to Charles. It was the incarcerated Lovelace who pointed out that stone walls do not a prison make, nor iron bars a cage. And it was Lovelace, explaining to his beloved Lucrasta why he had to go to war, who famously begged:

Tell me not (Sweet) I am unkind
That from the nunnery
Of thy chaste breast, and quiet mind,
To war and arms I flie.
True; a new mistress now I chase,
The first foe in the field;
And with a stronger faith embrace
A sword, a horse, a shield.
Yet this inconstancy is such,
As you too shall adore;
I could not love thee (Dear) so much,
Loved I not honour more.

The Tate Gallery does not have the pictures to do justice to the William Dobson who captured this unbearably romantic *High Noon* mood so perfectly. But they do exist. The Marquess of Northhampton owns a magnificent Dobson full length of Sir William Compton, aged 18, with a red satin sash across his tunic, which goes with his red breeches, and with the fiery tints of the big sunset behind. Compton died young as well. Cromwell called him the "godly cavalier". He was 17 when he enlisted in his father's regiment to fight the roundheads. At the siege of Banbury he charged the enemy on eleven unsuccessful occasions. Dobson painted him in 1643, in Oxford, where the king was in exile, and captured the full swagger of Compton as well as his fledgling sorrow. The elegant full lengths of Gainsborough and Reynolds are a century and half away. But they are being prefigured with extravagant aplomb. Isn't British art supposed to be gauche and clumsy and primitive at this particular moment in its history? Wasn't it looking to foreigners to raise its standards?

Dobson was an exquisite capturer of that English mix of ancient insolence and youthful

'Portrait of the
Artist with
Nicholas Lanier
and Sir Charles
Cotterell',
c.1638 – "the
first major
self-portrait
in British art
produced by
the first keen
British self-
portraitist"

courage that fired the cavalier spirit. If I ever have a chance to have a one to one with Earl Spencer, I will ask him if the cocky Dobson portrait of Colonel John Russell that hangs in Althorp gave him the emotional backing he needed to stand up in Westminster Abbey, in full view of the censorious world, and say what needed to be said on the occasion of his sister's funeral. Dobson's Russell in Althorp is only a half length. But he stares down at you from a great psychological height with spectacular arrogance.

The same sitter makes another fine Dobsonesque appearance in one of the most innovative compositions ever produced by an English hand. It was painted in around 1643 and shows three cavalier heroes, Russell, Prince Rupert and Colonel William Murray, gathered around a table to pledge a mysterious royalist oath. Murray dips his cockade in a glass of wine. The other two look on. It is sometimes assumed that Dobson learned everything from Van Dyck – how to paint satins, silks, and youthful assurance; how to employ Venetian colours and attempt elegant poses – but Van Dyck never produced a scene filled with as much psychological and historical tension as Dobson's evocation of this obscure moment in civil war history. Indeed, no one, anywhere, painted scenes like these. They are portraiture and history painting rolled into one. The fierce wind of history picked up a superb native portraitist and tossed him in strange directions.

The Tate also does not have the pictures to celebrate or reveal the gripping cavalier painting of William Dobson. The group portrait of Russell, Rupert and Murray is also in private hands. And thus, while the other historically crucial British Williams – Hogarth, Turner – will be given their due by a national collection packed with their produce, when the new gallery of British art opens at Millbank, Dobson will be overlooked because his pictures are scattered about the land in noble family homes and minor regional museums. Of the Tate's own holdings, only the celebrated portrait of Endymion Porter can be described as a Dobson masterpiece, although it is neither as stirring nor, indeed, as typical as some of the doomed Dobson hot-heads found elsewhere.

Probably painted in London before the forced royalist exodus to Oxford in 1642, the Porter picture highlights another of Dobson's gifts: bluntness. Here is an ageing and stocky Englishman with a ruddy outdoor complexion – again, so un-Van Dyckian – who finds himself recorded in a colour scheme as full of nut browns and autumn oranges as a Suffolk wood in November. What an unusual and gorgeous English colour scheme it is.

When Van Dyck painted Porter – one of Charles I's most excellent courtiers – he slimmed him down, gave him a contrapposto pose to assume, and recorded him as an elegant London fixer. Dobson sends him back

into the countryside with his hunting rifle, pours some port down him and turns him back into a gentleman farmer. Endymion Porter's stocky frontality disappeared from British art for a century, until Hogarth rediscovered it with his great portrait of Captain Coram. Dobson found it first. He was also the first – and this was a move of intuitive genius – to employ a meaningfully square canvas that seemed, somehow, to ground his older sitters in blunter Englishness: to emphasise their solidity and frontality. And while we're making temporal comparisons with Hogarth, who can miss the earthy wenchiness of Dobson's portrait of his second wife, Judith, with her Covent Garden stare and that fabulous expanse of big bosom. Quick hands painted her, and can be felt enjoying so much life in her. She is the first in a line of splendid British wenches and shrimp girls whose presence in art is as fresh as a sea breeze.

No one knows for sure where Dobson learned how to do all this. He seems to have studied initially under William Peake, the son of James I's sergeant painter, Robert Peake, a typical London provincial and producer of well-dressed doll figures that never lost their Tudor stiffness. Whatever it was that Dobson learned from the Peakes he soon forgot, thank heavens. Van Dyck would have been a powerful influence, of course. And it also appears that Dobson may have been involved with Francis Cleyn in designing tapestries for the famous Mortlake factory, in which case he

would have known, intimately, the Raphael cartoons for the Sistine Chapel tapestries, which can still be seen at the V&A.

I have been listing various important achievements of Dobson's, and suggesting reasons why he has been underrated. But there is one set of historical circumstances that undoubtedly helped to make him the exceptional artist he was – before civil war and decrepitude got to him – that had nothing to do with his talents: he was merely lucky to be alive at the right time. For it could be said that the Renaissance came late to Britain. It arrived in the age of Charles I, and, for a few pre-Cromwell years of art buying and cultural ostentation, the British court was the most enlightened in Europe. Dobson was the only native artist to draw succour from this short yet splendid interval.

These days, after two centuries of Windsor dullness, it is almost impossible to imagine a royal family that was not only fond of progressive art, but which also insisted that the state be visibly supportive of that art. It certainly happened under the second Stuart. To a very real extent, Charles's love of art precipitated the civil war, for it was the spectacle of so much national resource being – as the roundheads saw it – squandered on the work of foreign painters that fuelled the crisis. Charles was beheaded not only as a lover of Catholics but also as a lover of art. Yet what a lover he was. To get some sense of the art that was available for viewing by Dobson in the royal collection, I recommend a trip to the Prado in Madrid. Go to the great central Titian gallery and, as you pan around the dozens of important Venetian masterpieces collected here, think to yourself: most of these were in Britain once. Charles, a particular lover of Venetian art, imported a staggering quantity of important Italian Renaissance paintings into London. The Raphaels, the Mantegnas, the da Vincis, the Titians and Veroneses – the first biography of Dobson insists that Charles called him the English Tintoretto – were displayed in the various royal palaces that Inigo Jones and his team were busily refurbishing and building to house them.

Dobson produced a noble portrait of the neurotic scholar charged with cataloguing this royal collection, Abraham van der Doort, which can now be found in the Hermitage in St Petersburg. Heaven knows how it got there. It proves that Dobson was as comfortable with introspective ancients as he was with fresh-faced cavaliers. Shortly after it was painted van der Doort committed suicide, and Dobson records him as an exceptionally troubled old man with downcast eyes. He also painted a famous Inigo Jones that belongs, I believe, to the Department of the Environment (it hangs in Chiswick House). It is one of so many crucial Dobson depictions that have ended up scattered about the corners of Britain by those mad winds of seventeenth-century history.

As a member of the circles of van der Doort and Inigo Jones, Dobson would have had intimate access to the royal collection, and therefore to the most spectacular gathering of Renaissance art outside Italy. We need look no further for the reasons behind the exceptional up-to-the-minute-ness of his vision, and for that sense you get in his presence of British art pole-vaulting from backward provincialism to sophisticated Europeanism in one spectacular progression.

There is something British as well about his decline. Loyally following the king to Oxford, Dobson can be seen running out of materials, enthusiasm and steam, as the tide of the great

Facing up to a fresh view of history. Facing page: 'An Old and a Younger Man', c.1640 (top); and 'Portrait of a Lady, half length', c.1640. Right: 'Endymion Porter', c.1642-1645

war turned against his side. His painting becomes sloppier and quicker. The paint surface grows thinner and thinner. More of his pictures remain unfinished. The vibrancy fades from the sashes of his cavaliers. A sad palette of greys and browns begins to dominate. And you never see what colour the breeches of his cavaliers might be because the grand full lengths are a thing of the past. The misery he records in a long set of scratchy heads and shoulders of the former heroes of war is grim and recurring. By 1646 he was dead. He was 35.

But that is not where I want to leave him. There is a chance that upon sneaking back into London after the fall of Oxford, Dobson painted one final masterpiece. As with most of his works, the self-portrait with Sir Charles Cotterell and (probably) Nicholas Lanier that now belongs to the Duke of Northumberland is impossible to date accurately. With Dobson, too much happened, too quickly. But it seems to be a late work. What is certain is that it is the first major self-portrait in British art produced by the first keen British self-portraitist.

There are two other self-portraits by Dobson, and they show a genuinely glamourous artistic presence fascinated by itself. With his long black locks and flamboyant moustache, Dobson had a cavalierish air of his own. The Duke of Northumberland's group portrait shows the artist embracing his patron, Sir Charles Cotterell, and turning his back on Lanier –

described by the era's best chronicler, George Vertue, as a "lusty grosse man" – while simultaneously fixing us with a marvellously direct stare that says: Look at me; see the choice I have made. The composition is based on a Veronese painting in Charles's collection (and now in the Frick in New York) in which Hercules is seen ostentatiously deciding between Pleasure and Virtue, and plumping for Virtue, naturally. In his great self-portrait, Dobson casts himself, modestly, in the Hercules role.

Has anyone out there ever seen a picture like this anywhere else in art? It bears some resemblance to the dark and charged half length gatherings of plotting musicians observed first by Giorgione and then by Titian. And the influence of Caravaggio – the Walker Art Gallery in Liverpool has a fine copy by Dobson of a Caravaggiesque night scene painted in Rome by Mattias Stomer – may explain some of the psychological complication that can be felt here. But these are no more than vague echoes. This remains an exceptional painting with no parallels of any kind in British art. In his *Brief Lives*, John Aubrey describes his contemporary, William Dobson, as "the most excellent painter that England hath yet bred". But Dobson was more than that. He was one of the most excellent painters that England would ever breed. And I look forward with real interest to seeing how the new independent home of British art at Millbank sets about rediscovering and rating him.

The word made sculpture

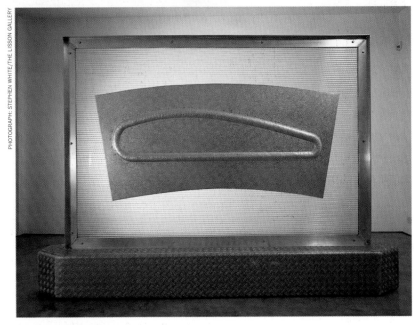

PHOTOGRAPH: STEPHEN WHITE/THE LISSON GALLERY

**Beyond surface values.
Above: 'The Interior is Always
More Difficult', 1992. Right:
Richard Deacon in his London
studio, 1998**

PHOTOGRAPH: PHIL SAYER

For the past two decades, Richard Deacon has been a major British sculptor with a substantial international reputation. As Tate Gallery Liverpool prepares to stage Deacon's first big show in Britain for ten years, director Lewis Biggs talks to the artist about his recent work, public sculpture, material culture, politics and an ongoing interest in the spoken and written word

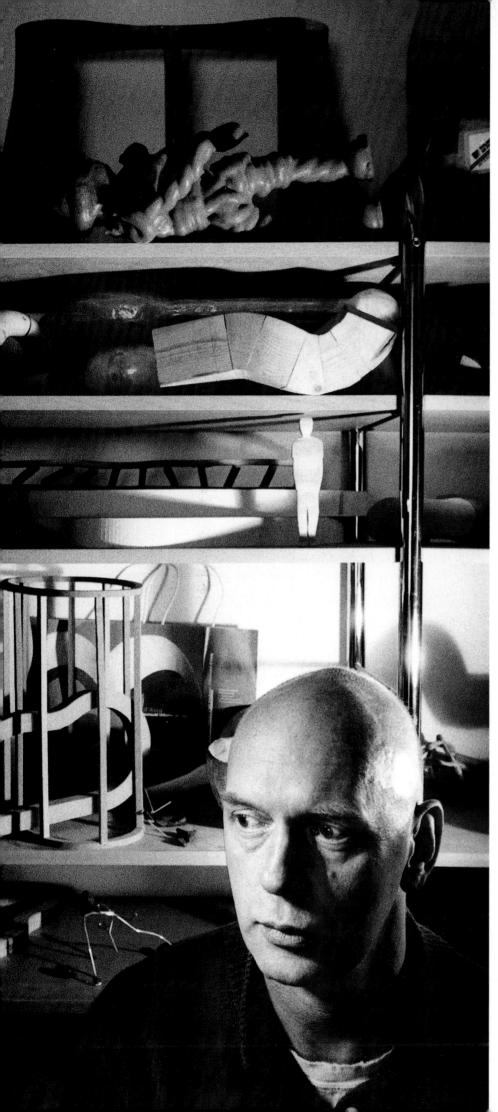

Lewis Biggs: *Since 1991, your work has been shown around the world, not least in major exhibitions in Germany – in Krefeld and Hanover in particular – but it is still largely unknown in this country. Why have you chosen the title "New World Order" for your show at Tate Gallery Liverpool, which features work made over the past ten years?*

Richard Deacon: There's a raft of reasons. In the past few years, I've tended to think of my work as being neither abstract nor representational, but somehow showing a different sort of world. Previously, I had emphasised metaphoric or allusive qualities in the work, which I think are still there, but less so.

Literal qualities have always been as important as the metaphoric qualities...

Yes, that's true, but (without wanting to sound too *X-files*, or too *Alien Resurrection* or whatever) if I'm making a landscape, I'm not making a representation of an existing landscape as much as a new landscape. So the title might have been "Another World Order". Also, it's not to do with fantasy. There's a certain amount of forward-looking Utopianism, or imagined others, implicit in the work.

What do you mean by fantasy? Fantasy is unreal, whereas what you make is real.

I didn't want to associate what I am saying too closely with the fantastic, or with *fin-de-siècle* symbolism. Fantasy is not a bad word. The second reason would be that the phrase "new world order" is definitely associated with George Bush and the Gulf War, and there's a synchronicity between his introduction of the phrase into wide currency and the dating of the works in the show. It's interesting that language comes to be like an object or to describe a condition. "New world order" operates as a nugget of language which contains an ideology, circumscribing a world view. I've often used language in the work as a means of trying to point out how the ways we talk about the world and the ways we think about the world are not entirely disassociated from the way the world looks. Somehow there's a certain symbiosis between the two. "New world order" seems to belong to that language-become-object category. I'm attempting, in the title of the show, to take hold of that object and, if not directly to question it, at least to address the intellectual processes involved in forming a world view. So it does have a sharpness, but in other ways it's a meaningless phrase. I think it's interesting how a meaningless phrase becomes almost like a weapon.

Many people have suggested there's an ironic aspect to your work: is one intention of the title to foreground irony or satire?

Actually it wasn't. I have a certain anger about the claim for a "new world order" that was not *my* world order. And it might quite simply reflect a need to irritate. I'm not constructing a satire, I'm trying to reclaim a world view, but to do so in the presence of reality and not sealed off from reality. But the work is capable of multiple propositions.

Yes, because there is always playfulness in the work. Play inevitably produces new solutions all the time, it's about shuffling the cards and producing something new. But that doesn't sit very easily with the anger, which is more direct. [Silence.] I didn't want to get you in the psychiatrist's chair...

There is a Freud quote from *Beyond the Pleasure Principle* when Freud describes imitative play as a means of mastering the environment. When I was thinking about the constellation of realism, mimesis, representation... yes, play does present new solutions, but it's also a way of describing the world.

Or of calling the world into being...

Yes, and of transforming the world, in that you make things stand for other things.

Could we talk more specifically about what's in the show and why?

The show starts with an "empty room", defined by the positioning of the series of seven drawings on translucent plastic screens in aluminium frames called 'The Interior is Always More Difficult'. Beginning with this series provides a location for the exhibition as a whole. The work is either inside the room, outside it, or on these screens. It provides a kind of model "environment". Because it's not just the drawings, it's also the screens and the aluminium frames which together act as a key or a coda for the other elements within the exhibition. As you go into this "empty room", to the left are the smaller works ['Art for Other People'] across the floor, which are materially, structurally and formally very diverse, and which you perambulate. To the right is a group of much more bulky objects, which block the way, and all of which are enclosed.

Volumetric?

And hermetic... except one which leans against the wall. And then, in the rooms with higher ceilings overlooking the river, there's a sequence of three large wooden structures. They are very different, but their material structure and their volume are wrapped together in each case, so the space and the volume the work occupies are both empty and full at the same time. The wood of which they are constructed is present throughout the object (this is particularly true of 'Laocoon') and occupies the space, but at the same time there is a hollowness which also occupies the space. So that whereas in the first galleries both the smaller and the bigger works "are" material skins...

... in the higher gallery the larger works have space inter-penetrating freely.

The works in this show are materially very specific and formally quite complex (and the things they resemble, the things to which they refer, or look like, are much less clear), so that they have this high clarity as "made objects".

The analogies are reduced?

There are some analogies, but reduced. The openness they have refers back to the "empty room", where the two conditions of form and material presence are signalled in the window drawings. The conditions are present in the same surface, but they're not mixed: it's a drawn shape on a plastic window within a frame. So the three-dimensional works in some ways actualise those conditions. The "windows" are not drawings for objects. When I first installed them in Krefeld I thought they were sculptures which had been fragmented into component parts and yet the component parts were still present in the same place. The subsequent works are like reassemblies of those components. That's why the windows are at the beginning of the exhibition. There are other things which I think are of interest in their in-between state: their transparency and the ways in which they are both to be looked through and at, at the same time. They obviously describe

this process more programmatically than the sculptures, although that is also an aspect of what the sculptures do.

I'm struck by the way your work has evolved in the past decade. The development visible in the large bent wood works ('Laocoon', 'What Could Make Me Feel This Way A', 'After') is the way in which space is allowed to flow through them, netted, perhaps, but not contained by them. They're highly complex in form, made out of repeated units which set up rhythms and intervals so that they seem composed less of shapes than of energy. On the other hand, they've also retained the attractive quality of many of your earlier works, in that they invite close inspection. They are intimate despite their large size. But in the galleries overlooking the dock, there will be a num-

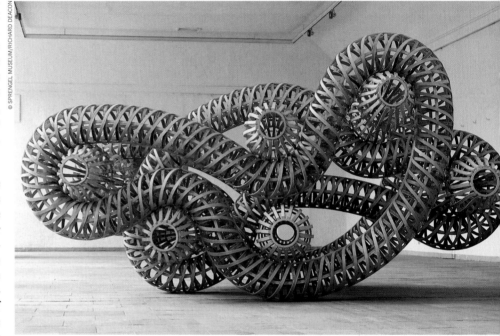

© SPRENGEL MUSEUM/RICHARD DEACON

© RICHARD DEACON

ber of works which are less attractive, even slightly repellent in their surface — literally repellent in the sense of shininess, or the reflective surface of plastic or glass.

They're more hermetic. The works from the 1980s tend to be structured in a different kind of a way. Their particulate nature is more evident, and so the rhetoric of all the detail of their assembly is part and parcel of what you see. Funnily enough, I think that the new wooden works are more mechanical than the hermetic works, which have a greater plasticity. Hollowness has been a significant feature, too, enclosing a shape completely and not allowing any entry point. Towards the end of the 1980s, I became dissatisfied with the necessary consequences of bending and folding, the kind of form making that bending and folding allows you to do, and began to look for a more fluid form, without wanting to make a solid.

At the end of the 1980s you made a large number of

sculptures for placement out of doors. Did this have an effect on the way in which your work developed?

The first one I made especially to go outdoors was in Liverpool, for the Garden Festival in 1984, although it was only a temporary work. Then there was a rush of work of this kind for me at the end of the 1980s. It made me think a lot about the notion of the "public". I had a certain amount of anger as well, not so much in the beginning, but it developed into a polemic against the appropriation of public space. I wrote a piece with Lynne Cooke at the beginning of the 1990s. It was just after the Berlin Wall had come down, and there were all those photographs of toppled monuments. I imagined, if the situation had been reversed, which monuments would have been destroyed. I wondered about the relationship between the monument and the public place. Sculpture was often seen as a decorative element within the public place and I was trying to assert that, to the contrary, it was a kind of guarantee of publicness. It had meanings in public, not in the sense of social engineering but in the proper political sense. I also wanted the work not to be governed by... Let's be arrogant. I thought sculpture came first. It preceded the gallery and the museum. Sculptures were being allowed to "be" only within the context of the museum, whereas in fact the museum was there only because those things were there. The constraints of this museum-orientated situation were inhibiting the capacity of the public to engage with sculpture publicly. So the rush of the work in the late 1980s and early 1990s was in part a consequence of opportunity, but also in part a consequence of my wish to engage with this debate.

The studio work may go to a museum or a private house; you have little control over where it ends up, and to that extent no control over its meanings. The 'Art for Other People' works were intended to be autonomous, and intimate wherever they were.

On the other hand, public sculpture, because it's fixed by its nature to a specific site, offers a whole new range of possibilities for engaging with meaning. Did you experience this as a liberation?

Yes, although I now find I get a lot of invitations to make proposals from people who know what they want and imagine that I will give it to them. At the moment I am mostly refusing the invitations. My interests have moved. I don't want to make very large sculptures... A year ago I was thinking I wanted to make tiny things, but the most fruitful area, and the most difficult one for me, is to make middle-sized, sculpture-sized sculptures. In the early 1980s I deliberately rejected that as a size because it seemed to bring too much with it in terms of history, context or whatever. I now think it is the most open area. Also, it's the most evacuated area. No one is trying to deal with it. It seems I have a certain kind of fluidity or comfort in making quite large objects, but what I'm interested in now is relatively modest scale objects. I am beginning to get very suspicious of installation, of site specificity, of those seemingly liberating notions about practice. In the mid-1980s and early 1990s, the public place was very liberating for me; it gave me confidence. At the moment it seems to be an overly

Organic food for thought. Clockwise from top right: 'Art for Other People 39', 1997; 'Plant', 1995; 'Like a ship', 1984 (in the foreground), 'Like a bird', 1984 (behind); 'What Could Make Me Feel This Way', 1993

complex way of making work: there are too many negotiations you have to go through. I'm not antagonistic to the ideology of it, but the critical engagement with it has somehow shifted away from the art and into the "field".

That's interesting, because up until ten years ago the range of analogy which was brought to bear on your work was basically from the language of the body, most particularly the ears, eyes and internal organs, and domestic instruments – the pots and pans. You moved away from that, but now you are saying that actually it's the body that interests you again. Well, perhaps not the body, but anything mid-size relates primarily to the body. Is it in any sense a move back to where you were?

Well, I didn't think it was... And I'm not sure that your assertion is correct. There's a size that is smaller than the body which doesn't refer to the body.

Like 'Beauty and the Beast'? That size?

Yes. I made a show earlier this year in which there was one 'Beauty and the Beast'. Part of the difficulty I had in the past was that when you get to a mid-sized sculpture you always see a body there. But I have begun to think that maybe there doesn't have to be. I find that very exciting as a possibility. In that sense it doesn't seem to me to be stepping backwards.

At the end of the 1980s, you seemed to be following several different strands in the work. One was about subjectivity and otherness, which is perhaps most manifest in the inside/outside theme. Another was an exploration of structure in a very holistic sense, looking at the world of objects from a structural point of view: what is it all made of? The works which address this most clearly are the 'Beauty and the Beast' made from folded cardboard, 'Laocoon', or 'What Could Make Me Feel This Way A'. These feel like something microscopic which has been enlarged. As opposed to domestic instruments or bodies, or sense analogies, the analogies these works appear to conjure are for the energy paths which produce structures.

Which are then materialised. We can go right back to the beginning and say that structure is undoubtedly a part of the "new world order". If you can bring structure into the frame as a carrier or a component in the search for meaning, if you can make structure an issue, then you also initiate an engagement with how the world is. In the past I think I've used structure as assembly; I've often talked about structure as a component in the work. Whereas the structure you're talking about now is more to do with materialisation than with assembly.

Yes, more to do with how to feel the world, or imagine the world, than how to assemble an object.

In a sense some of the sculptures are to do with something like an externalisation, a manifestation.

Maybe it's important to talk about individual sculptures. What is it that they are manifesting?

Well, that's more problematic... It could be that they are just about nothing.

That hasn't been the way you have worked.

I made some works about the idea of the beautiful, and I have made works about ideas of libertarianism and authoritarianism... such as 'Nothing is Forbidden' and 'Nothing is Allowed'.

Maybe analogy is the wrong tree to be barking up. Maybe the work is less analogous, more something else...

Yes, I think that's true, but you still have to answer the question as to what the something else is.

More metaphoric. Analogy has simile in it, whereas

metaphor allows for the complete disjunction of the object from the original source of energy which suggested the object. Dealing with more abstract issues produces more abstract sculptures…

I suppose I would say that the issues are more abstract, but the means are more concrete. There's material specificity and a multiplicity of means. The material is obviously manipulated, but less overtly than before, less descriptively – that's the word, less descriptively– which leaves you in the funny position where the work is performing negative functions but at the same time being positively present. It's not a particular image, it's not this, it's not that, so a certain kind of negativity or negation is used. And also transparency (it plays a part there somewhere) is used as a way of trying to represent a formal subjectivity.

You were reported as having said that "the nexus of meaning is itself perhaps illusory". Referring to the sculpture as a "nexus of meaning" seems a perfectly sensible and logical thing to do. Was this a moment of pessimism or depression on your part? [Deacon laughs]. *Or was that not what you were saying?*

No, that was what I was saying. I think it is possible to doubt. I think it's possible for objects to carry meaning, and I don't think it's necessarily the case that they always do. I used to say a long time ago that I made sculpture because it was a way of looking at the world, and sculpture acted as a kind of screen. What I was interested in was that it was an in-between fact, it wasn't me and it wasn't the world, it was between the two of us. The notion of the in-between has sociability built into it, hence my interest in language. And also to some extent my interest in public work. I gave a rather stupid version of it just now, but actually it's to do with sociability, and the consequences of that being in between us. I still think that's what I do when I make sculpture. I use it as an

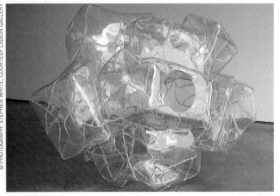

in-between. What I think has changed is that a number of the sculptures I made in the 1980s used that in-between and then themselves constructed a metaphor for the act of perception, the acts of apprehension, through the organs. So there was a complicity between the organ and the experience, in a material form. The subject was apprehension and apprehension of the world. Progressively, I've become seemingly less interested in that than in the constitution of a world. I still think that sociability mediates through that in-between notion, between my fingers and sociability. In recent interviews I think I have tended to over-emphasise the material.

It has to be counter-balanced by your interest in the cerebral. That's what happened. In the 1980s it was more hand to mouth to eye… now it's more brain work.

Brain to material. Back in 1983 I did that thing called "Making Sculpture" on the lawn at the Tate. I was next to Michael Pennie. Michael started with a very large piece of wood, and I started with some sheets of steel stacked up at the back. I was very interested in the way that the more he did the less there was, and the more I did the more there was. And in the notion of the will in relation to that: the thing I made was more willed than what he made. He seemed to take away something basic, something brutal from the object, and replace it with something else.

So carving is less "willed" than constructing?

He started with a massive piece of wood; with an incredibly strong physical presence as an object. Something disappeared, which was the object. The object disappeared and was replaced by something else. There was no object before I started, and there was at the end. So I thought I had an object and an image, whereas Michael took away some

sense of identity, some presence, which was a consequence of this physical mass. By removing the mass you do remove something. You could look at that as a historical question. Why Michelangelo's 'Slaves' are interesting is because they are imprisoned. Rodin is also engaged with that problematic at some points.

You were once involved in an architectural project with Richard Rogers.

We made a film, directed by John Tchalenko, after the Serpentine show in 1985, about Pierre Charreau's house. It was the time that Richard Rogers was making the Lloyd's building, and he was describing how he used the Maison de Verre as a model for the building. I thought it was interesting because – for a modernist icon – the architecture itself seemed to be immensely referential. The house was far from being a machine, but had within it all kinds of references to other sorts of structures, so we talked about it in terms of symbolic architecture. For example, there are five staircases in the house, each one built differently. One is like a spiral staircase in a castle, another is like a hanging bridge in the Andes, another is like a drawbridge in a castle. It was interesting to find that level of experimentation, well, openness and indeterminacy, in a high modernist icon.

Architects have to deal with a far more circumscribed set of problems than the public sculptor has to. Maybe people's expectations are lower for architecture?

One of the differences between architecture and public sculpture is that architecture comes with a brief. One of the problems with public sculpture is *when* it comes with a brief! Artists aren't good at working to briefs. That lack of function, the absence of a brief in the strict sense, is a positive virtue, but it doesn't imply that anything goes. It has to make sense.

"Richard Deacon: New World Order", sponsored by the Henry Moore Foundation, Tate Gallery Liverpool, 20 February-16 May

In the eye of the beholder. Above: 'Almost Beautiful', 1994. Left: 'Beauty and the Beast A', 1995

The Ashbourne Gallery

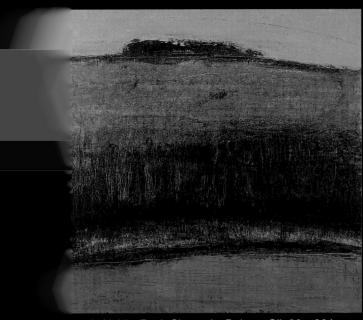

Lewis Noble, Rush Channels, Dalyan. Oil, 36 x 36 in

Richard Wallace, Resting Figure, Oil, 12 x 12 in

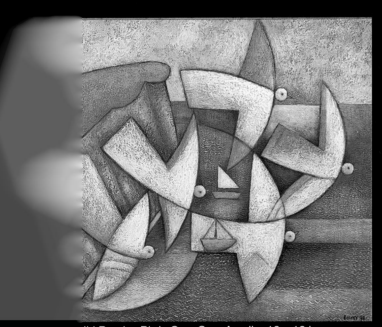

Jiri Borsky, Birds Over Sea. Acrylic, 16 x 16 in

Charlotte Mayer, Journey (ii). Bronze, height 39 in

Major solo shows for 1999 include:

Michael Porter – January

Lewis Noble – April

Charlotte Mayer – June

Elizabeth Ridgway – September

Regular exhibitors include:

Noel Betowski, Jiri Borsky, Jon Buck, Shelley Caines, Sue Campion, Henrietta Corbett, Simon Hart, Graham
Kurt Jackson, Andrew Macara, Stephen Todd, Patricia Volk, Richard Wallace.

Gallery	50 St. John Street, Ashbourne, Derbyshire DE6 1GH
Open	Tues-Sat 10am – 5.30 pm
Tel	+44 (0) 1335 346742
Fax	+44 (0) 1335 347101
Email	treg.fineart@dial.pipex.com
Web	http://dspace.dia.pipex.com/treg.fineart

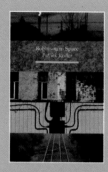
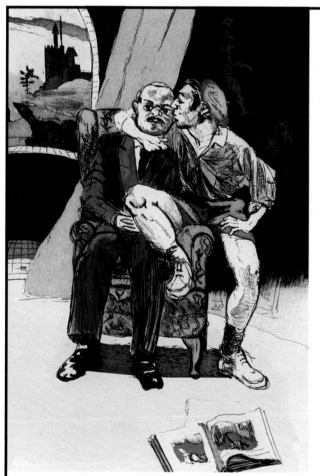

Get into the Tate

and enjoy...

Free entry to all Tate Gallery exhibitions in London, Liverpool and St Ives

Including: **Jackson Pollock (Spring 1999)**
Abracadabra: International Contemporary Art (Summer 1999)
The Art of Bloomsbury (Winter 1999)

Free subscription to *tate: the art magazine* – normal cover price £3.50

Our special London and Liverpool Friends Rooms where you can relax with like-minded art lovers

And the satisfaction of knowing you are supporting one of the world's leading galleries.

Join now
Call 0171-887 8752 or fill in the form opposite

www.tate.org.uk
Friends of the Tate Gallery is a registered charity, number 313021.

Supported by
TATE & LYLE

The power of Pollock

Win – a silk-screen print of Jackson Pollock's 'Summertime', 1948, produced by King and McGaw to celebrate the Pollock exhibition at the Tate Gallery and worth £80. 'Summertime' was painted in his studio on Long Island and is one of a number of highly abstract works that relates to the seasons and evokes the vastness of the American landscape.

Win – one of five *Jackson Pollock* catalogues by Kirk Varnedoe, Chief Curator of Painting and Sculpture at the Museum of Modern Art, New York. It accompanies the first retrospective in more than 30 years of one of the most influential American painters of the twentieth century.

Win – *Interpreting Pollock* by Jeremy Lewison, Director of Collections at the Tate Gallery.

Simply answer the question and complete the form on the back of this card

© TATE GALLERY, ARS, NY, DACS, LONDON 1999

To join us...

First choose basic membership...

£24 Membership As a member, you will enjoy free admission to all exhibitions at the Tate in London, Liverpool and St Ives (including the Barbara Hepworth Museum). You will receive three editions of *tate: the art magazine* each year – and save £10.50 on the cover price.

You can use the Friends Rooms in both London and Liverpool to relax in peace and calm.

You will receive regular updates on what is happening at the Tate, and invitations to a range of events – from lectures by experts to special visits.

As a member, you can also decide which of the following benefits you wish to add to your membership. Simply tick the appropriate box or boxes on the form opposite.

... then choose what you would like to add on

£12 Guest pass Accompanied by you, your guest will enjoy unlimited admission to all exhibitions at the Tate in London, Liverpool and St Ives. They will also benefit from privileged access to the Friends Rooms in London and Liverpool.

£18 Family pass Your family pass gives one guest and any of your children under 18 unlimited admission to all exhibitions at the Tate in London, Liverpool and St Ives. They will also benefit from privileged access to the Friends Rooms in London and Liverpool.

£12 London private view pass/late pass Around six times a year, you and a guest will be invited to one of our special evening private views of exhibitions and the permanent collection.

£6 Liverpool and/or St Ives package For an additional £6 a year, your benefits at either Tate Gallery St Ives (including the Barbara Hepworth Museum) or Tate Gallery Liverpool will include invitations to private views, as well as news on local events and activities. You'll also be able to take a guest along whenever you visit.

... simply fill in this form

Please tick the appropriate box or boxes opposite to indicate the membership benefits you wish to enjoy.

☑ **Membership £24**

Then choose from:

☐ **Guest pass £12** (all three galleries)
☐ **Family pass £18** (all three galleries)
☐ **London private view pass/ late pass £12**
☐ **St Ives package £6**
☐ **Liverpool package £6**

Additional donation £ _____

TOTAL £ _____

Mr/Mrs/Ms/Miss _____

Address _____

Postcode _____ **Telephone** _____

Date of birth _____

I enclose a cheque for £ _____ (payable to Friends of the Tate Gallery)

OR Please debit my MasterCard/Visa/EuroCard/Switch* (circle one)

Number ☐☐☐☐ ☐☐☐☐ ☐☐☐☐ ☐☐☐☐ / ☐☐☐

* For Switch, please copy the long number from the middle of your card, and put the issue number opposite. **Issue number** (Switch only) ☐☐

Amount £ _____ **Expiry date** _____

Signature _____ **Date** _____

Credit card billing address (if different from above)

_____

☐ Please tick if you prefer not to receive communications from other carefully selected organisations.

Please return to: Membership Office, Tate Gallery, FREEPOST, London SW1P 4BR

Friends of the Tate Gallery is a registered charity, number 313021.

Subscribe to *tate*

Please begin a subscription to *tate: the art magazine*

☐ One-year 3-issues: £9.45 United Kingdom (saving 10%);
   £20 Overseas; $29 United States

☐ Two-year 6-issues: £18 United Kingdom (special offer);
   £32 Overseas; $49 United States

Mr/Mrs/Ms/Miss _____

Full Address _____

_____

Postcode _____ Telephone _____

I enclose a cheque for £ _____ (payable to Blueprint Media Ltd)

Please debit my Access/Visa/EuroCard/ArtsCard (circle as appropriate)

Number ☐☐☐☐☐☐☐☐☐☐☐☐☐☐☐☐

Amount £ _____ Expiry Date _____

Please advise if credit card address is different from above

_____

_____

Signature _____ Date _____

Please return this form to:
tate Subscriptions, FREEPOST 11 (WD 4260), London W1E 2JZ

The power of Pollock

1ST PRIZE Jackson Pollock 'Summertime' silk-screen print worth £80.
2ND PRIZE five *Jackson Pollock* catalogues worth £50.
RUNNER-UP PRIZES ten copies of *Interpreting Pollock* worth £9.99.

To enter the competition simply answer the question and send your completed form to Philip Allison, tate, Avon House, Kensington Village, Avonmore Road, London, W14 8TS.

QUESTION: Who will be playing Jackson Pollock in the forthcoming film of his life?
Answer _____

Name _____

Address _____

_____

Postcode _____

TERMS AND CONDITIONS
1. Every correct entry form received before the closing date will be put into the draw.
2. Closing date for the competition is 08.03.99.
3. No purchase necessary.
4. Winners will be notified within 28 days.
5. Employees and families of Aspen or Tate Gallery Publishing are not eligible to enter.
6. No responsibility can be accepted for non delivery or lateness of entries.
7. Winners names can be obtained by sending a SAE to Tate, Avon House, Kensington Village, London W14 8TS.

Get into the Tate

Join now call
0171-887 8752
or fill in the form overleaf

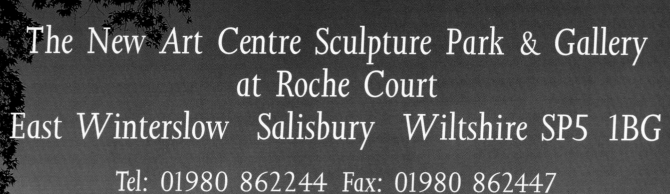

The New Art Centre Sculpture Park & Gallery
at Roche Court
East Winterslow Salisbury Wiltshire SP5 1BG
Tel: 01980 862244 Fax: 01980 862447
e-mail: nac@globalnet.co.uk

A new gallery designed by
Munkenbeck+Marshall
has just opened at Roche Court.

In the sculpture park, there are over
a hundred works by 20th century sculptors.

Open every day all year round: 11am — 4pm

terry winters
and henri michaux

19 February - 25 April 1999

Next to Aldgate East
Open Tues-Sun, 11am-5pm
(Wed till 8pm)
Admission free
Recorded information:
0171-522 7878

AKELER

A-AA

Institut Français

the whitechapel art gallery

BARBICAN ART GALLERY

29 January–28 March 1999
Barbican Art Gallery
Barbican Centre, London EC2
Barbican, Moorgate
Information 0171 588 9023

Picasso

Picasso & Photography: The Dark Mirror

Gjon Mili, *Picasso Drawing with the Pencil of Light*, 1949. Picasso Archives, Musée Picasso, Paris

YORKSHIRE
SCULPTURE PARK
BRETTON HALL
WEST BRETTON
WAKEFIELD
WEST YORKSHIRE

TEL +44 (0)1924 830302

FAX +44 (0)1924 830044

ADMISSION FREE

GROUNDS OPEN DAILY 10-4
GALLERIES/CAFE 11-4
INFORMATION CENTRE 10-4

1 MILE FROM M1 JUNCTION 38

KINGS CROSS - WAKEFIELD 2 HRS

EXHIBITIONS AND PROJECTS SPRING 1999

JACQUES LIPCHITZ
Open-air and Pavilion Gallery
continuing until April 6

KIT
Internet project / CD ROM
http:www.ysp.co.uk

MULTIPLES STORE

HERMIONE WILTSHIRE

SHAUN PICKARD

HENRY MOORE IN
BRETTON COUNTRY PARK

YSP COLLECTION 1999 INCLUDES:

JAUME PLENSA . SERGE SPITZER
BARBARA HEPWORTH . GRENVILLE DAVEY
PHILLIP KING . ANTHONY CARO
DHRUVA MISTRY . JONATHAN BOROFSKY
JOANNA PRZYBYLA . SOL LEWITT
RICHARD SERRA . RICHARD ROME
DAVID NASH . EDWARD ALLINGTON

Estorick Collection

of modern italian art

ZANG

TUMB

TUMB

F. Depero: *Depero Futurista 1927*

THE FUTURIST GRAPHIC REVOLUTION

6 January - 11 April 1999

39a Canonbury Square
London N1 2AN
Highbury & Islington

Admission £2.50 (£1.50 concs.)
Wednesday - Saturday 11.00 - 18.00
Sunday 12.00 - 17.00

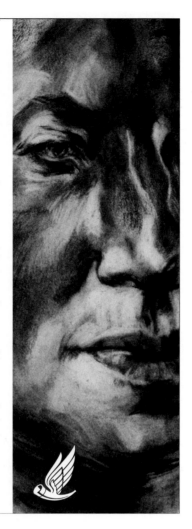

Insight

Books/Films/Television/Radio/CD-Roms

TELEVISION

The Truth About Art

Written and presented by
Waldemar Januszczak
Directed by Phil Stebbing
Channel 4 Television

Reviewed by Richard Wentworth

The Television People are the
hunter/gatherers of our time. They
bring us a continuum of things to
flicker in our well-appointed caves.
If the budget is big, they can bring
us big things over long distances.
They can even show us things in the
wonderfully named "real time", or
not. They can show us things for a
millisecond. Sometimes their
programmes are made to last, more
often not. Knowing that they don't
bring us a lot of art, I was excited to
see what Waldemar Januszczak would
be bringing me in his new series.

Waldemar loves his subject, and as
a commissioning editor at Channel 4
he must have surveyed an astonishing
amount of visual material, a kind of
critical luxury but also a terrifying
loss of innocence, a mighty
imposition, to have seen so much.
Hearing that his three broadcasts on
Sundays in December would be
called *The Truth About Art*, and
subtitled *Animals*, *Gods* and *Lovers*,
it was not difficult to imagine him
wishing to get back to basics,
proposing something plain speaking.
I guessed he wanted to be generous
to his audience, to spread the good
word. I still think of Sunday
broadcasting as having a moral
dimension… perhaps the programmes
would be good for me.

The titles, a pastiche of Terry
Gilliam's now 30-year-old animation
for *Monty Python*, seemed nostalgic
and silly, but as number one was
Animals, I guessed it might be the
Douanier Rousseau story, all foliage
and fear. *Animals* began with a
figure fossicking among dry leaves
and then disappearing into a hole in
the ground. This was the director's
device for introducing you (a) to
Waldemar and (b) to Lascaux in
south-west France. The caves at
Lascaux are a fine place to start, a
sort of entombed collective
unconscious. The fact that the
pictures are part and parcel of the
contorted surfaces of the caves, the
way the animals gather together and

separate, the dank and the dark, the
profound sense of secrecy and the
guaranteed metaphor of something
hidden being revealed, are great
readymades for any film director. Just
add patience and tact. Any sense of
wonder which might have been
imparted was instantly overtaken by
Januszczak confiding to camera.
Whispering in the style of David
Attenborough (animals, get it?), he
made the astoundingly suburban
observation that caves were dark and
scary and that blackness was spooky,
as if the Lascaux artists were using
his standards when they picked their
cave 20,000 years before – they'd
already tried the one with fitted

carpets and the other one with the
new damp course and running hot
water. Everybody knows that caves
are sexy. My concern for this
foolish comparison was interrupted
by a millisecond flash of a worse for
wear shark in a tank, set to the
sound of exaggerated bathwater,
and then instantaneously back to
base at Lascaux.

Back in the cave, WJ touched very
correctly on the question of light, but
it was the Duracell torch which had
to stand in for fire and, without so
much as a naked flame, we were off to
Africa to visit the bushmen in
southern Zimbabwe – 8,000 miles in
less than a second. This was our first

**Waldemar Januszczak tells 'The
Truth About Art'**

taste of the distances we could expect
to travel on the Januszczak budget,
moving across history and geography
much as we do when we watch the
news. Struggling to hold the ambition
and diversity of his material together,
Januszczak was going to be our
newsreader, to see us through. As
long as we had animals as our subject,
we could go anywhere – it was all fair
game. To Sellafield to look at mutant
bugs, to Innsbruck for the cabinet of
curiosities, to gentleman pig breeders
in Devon, to Parisian cemeteries to
look for dead artists (Soutine, not

Douanier Rousseau), to spoof museums in Los Angeles via Dutch morality painting. As the subject got pulled hither and thither it fell to the human animal to make the last links, and too much jokey newsreader is simply too much. The underlying sense of purpose was admirable – a chance to visit fear and desire, mortality, hunger and gluttony, sex and beauty, with taxonomy and acquisition as the pervading themes. Amongst it all there was a single, unforgettably authentic image of Januszczak crushing cochineal beetles between finger and thumb, the intense red pigment spreading out across his skin. Januszczak explained that without the beetle there would be no good reds in oil paint. The economy of this image was worth a thousand words.

Because television's art is to make its craft seamless, it is shy of trying to show that the world is actually made. If you can forget to make plain the power of a naked flame, you can just as easily forget to explain what economic forces extract a shark from the sea and put it in a tank. The great pleasure of Lascaux and the Zimbabwe rock paintings is that they are tied to their place. Our idea of art is that it is distributable, that we can reproduce it, move it around. On the rare occasions when art resists being moved, we simply transport ourselves to it. The sense of frenetic tourism in all these programmes was fatiguing precisely because it was never acknowledged. Occasionally, local experts would be summoned to try to nail down a subject, which lent parts of the programme an old world Open University charm. The exception was John Richardson in *Lovers*, whose performance was as deliciously louche as it was knowledgeable (about Picasso).

The director's taste for illustrative art direction was truly tacky – a snail placed on Soutine's enamelled photograph on his gravestone, getting Januszczak to paw a slimy clay model in the life room and persuading him to ogle women through a hole in a newspaper (Picasso style) were conspicuous low points. The live artists were used as a foil to the dead ones and were often very good. What they said was usually better than what the camera showed. Cornelia Hesse-Honegger, whose watercolours of mutant bugs suffered the click/flash/click/flash of the televised

slide show, spoke well of children being trained, not educated, and how the visual impulse was deadened for them. David Wilson in his fantasy museum in Los Angeles, like some distant tweedy relation of Gilbert & George, spoke well on "wonder". Down on the farm, Damien Hirst did a perfect impersonation of an autodidact farmboy. Of Soutine (the footballer) he said: "He went for it, and pulled it off."

In *Lovers*, Louise Bourgeois was magnificently fierce and chiding, while Jenny Savile, as antidote to John Richardson, was filmed art directing a gigantic pile of women's bodies. She talked of the warmth and smell and closeness of travelling in the tube, but the camera, ever courteous, never betrayed so much as a pulse beneath the skins of her models. Cindy Sherman had a small walk-on part as a chameleon. In her invisibility, Januszczak scolded her for being American and influential.

The tristesse of all this tourism does serve to remind us that context is still everything. We discover, at the end of *Animals*, that Lascaux is a concrete replica, a Whiteread for the appetite of us tourists, a piece of scenographic make believe. By a fluke of programming, WJ's *Gods* was followed, on another channel (BBC2), by Richard Billingham's *Fishtank*. Although this young artist had never intended his years of accumulated material for broadcasting, in the space of 50 minutes his work questioned every television value I took for granted seconds before it began. Animals, pets, lovers and dying flies. The Truth about Life. More living artists please.

PHAIDON PRESS

BOOK

CREAM

Edited by Gilda Williams et al
Phaidon, £29.95
Reviewed by Irit Rogoff

Three types of lists are identified in Jack Goody's now classic essay from 1977, "What's in a List?". Retrospective lists are an inventory of persons, objects or events; shopping lists serve as a guide to future action; and lexical lists are an inventory of concepts, a proto-dictionary or embryonic encyclopedia.

CREAM is a veritable orgy of list making, retrospective but claiming to be of the shopping variety. It selects ten curators who begin by listing writings by ten contemporary thinkers whose work they find significant for contemporary cultural discussions. The selections are too short for us to engage with any of the writers' actual complexity, so presumably they are there as a tease to produce a desire for more substantial reading. There is nothing at all wrong with the texts included in the lists: they are the texts that shape much of our contemporary thinking, that we teach at university, and all of them are good and important. There is, however, something fundamentally off in a project that ceaselessly and gratingly insists on "contemporaneity" and fails to understand that part of the challenge of post-modernity has been the

Fabián Marcaccio, 'Environment Paintant', 1997-1998

dissolution of canons and master influences and a notion of "the best".

The second and more substantial part of the book is devoted to 100 artists proposed by the same ten curators. The breadth of the work shown is welcome, and the examples chosen by virtually all of the curators – and by Rosa Martinez in particular – provide what one expects from such a project: to be informed of what is happening across several continents.

The overall aim was clearly an attempt at a culturally integrated practice – to combine the materials of a contemporary international art exhibition with those of contemporary university courses in critical theory and visual culture. In addition, we are provided with some reflections on their own practice and its limitations by prominent curators working within the international art market – all of these packaged into a portable exhibition space of contemporary culture. Yet one is left with a strong sense of the project's inadequacy. We have reflexive curators, snippets of important theoretical texts and lots of interesting young artists, so why doesn't it work?

While I have various design and typography quibbles with the book's format – its unwieldiness, that the work by the artists presented is overlaid by the words of the curators or framed by critical observations at one end and biographical information at the other – none of these is more than a trivial, irritable complaint. The real challenge of this tome is not the size of the table required to spread it out or an understanding of its indexical logic, but to try to tease out the vision of visual culture it is offering us. Perhaps because, in Goody's words, the lists have served to make everything more visible as well as more abstract in a way that is culturally without context.

Goody's argument is that the list form which appeared at the moment of the rise of written language in antiquity did not simply fill a need, but actually represented a significant change in "modes of thought" within these cultures, since information presented in lists must be processed in a different way. Lists rely on discontinuity, depend on physical placement, on location, can be read in different directions. They have boundaries rather than narrative structures and encourage ordering items by number, by initial sound, by

Insight

Ana Laura Aláez, 'Bubbles', 1996

category. Most importantly, says Goody, lists bring greater visibility to categories while at the same time making them more abstract.

In the context of *CREAM* that abstraction clearly has to do with a globalising decontextualisation of the work. The book produces a moveable feast of an international contemporary art world viewed through its circulations.

While I would never argue that context and intention can tie down meanings, I was acutely aware in those instances in which I was familiar with the work and its receptions that a certain flattening and equalisation had taken place within this circulatory mode which erased some of the initial shock of recognition that the work offered. I vividly remember the horrific encounter with Kara Walker's images of slavery stencilled on the walls of San Francisco MoMA and, even more vividly, the embarrassed discomfort of the viewers whose gaze was forced to engage with the work. It is not the absence of shock, or of horror, or the thrill of the new that I sorely miss here, but the recognition that it is the subjectivities of viewers which work to complete the process. To allow for that subjectivity to surface one needs space and tentativeness, neither of which can be achieved through audiences being bombarded with densely saturated visions of "new". Therefore, while one is grateful for the information and its democratising potential, we remain deeply excluded in terms of our own potential contribution to fleshing out the culture on display.

BOOK

Mark Rothko

Edited by Jeffrey Weiss
Yale University Press, £40
Reviewed by Stephen Polcari

The year 1998 was a problematic one in New York, with exhibitions of two of the premier American artists of the second half of the twentieth century, Mark Rothko and Jackson Pollock. It was the first major museum show of Rothko's work in America since the retrospective at the Guggenheim Museum in 1978 and was conceived to celebrate the publication of a seven-year project, David Anfam's splendid catalogue *raisonné*, *Mark Rothko/Works on Canvas* (Yale University Press and the National Gallery of Art, Washington, 1998). While the Pollock show is at the Tate, the Rothko can be seen at the Musée d'Art Moderne de la Ville de Paris (until 18 April).

The two celebrity artists are fundamental to the achievements and controversies of twentieth-century American painting, and both shows are wonderful as exhibits of their modernist positions. But that is their weakness as well as their strength, for neither takes many chances, preferring to concentrate on the greatest hits. The later, post-1947 work is emphasised as it always has been. For Rothko, what is on view is the transcendent colourism of his abstract, rectilinear stacks of ever-moving and tremulous rectangles; for Pollock, it is the sexiness of his pouring and dripping technique. The artists' entire careers are selected and edited to point to the great triumph of New York art: internationalist, modernist abstraction.

However, in a way, both shows take place at an unlucky moment – when the very ground upon which they rest has shifted. New scholars have provided fresh information, understandings and conceptualisations for Pollock's and Rothko's work. The exhibitions display awareness of these new ideas, but neither chooses to change traditional views. Both curators, Jeffrey Weiss at the National Gallery and Kirk Varnedoe at the Museum of Modern Art in New York, are from the same school, New York University's Institute of Fine Arts,

and have had little direct, personal engagement with the new scholarship. The result is a hardening of the establishment's view of the artists.

In the Rothko show, Weiss presents the new deepening of source, idea and theme that lies behind the work mostly in unacknowledging wall labels. However, his ill-at-ease establishment view is particularly evident in the catalogue, which holds to the tried and the true. Weiss has chosen to emphasise pictorial characteristics of the late work, that is, its form, space, surface and colour. He continues to concentrate on Rothko's abstractions and their formal qualities and achievements. In the essays, there is little discussion of the early work, the necessary element to understanding and grounding any complete concept of Rothko. New scholarship examines the early work which is most often termed "surrealist", but which Rothko himself called the "Greek figures". Rather than discussing formal elements yet again – we are in the fifth decade of such a discourse – it looks at the ideas and themes of the work, and the cultural and historical world from which it arises. In other words, recent thinking considers Rothko's work as a unified *oeuvre*, dominated by ideas from the specific cultural discourses of his era, and it recognises that his work and those ideas have historical and cultural sources and resonance, a concept not to be found in depth in Weiss's approach. This is a catalogue that is safe and not sorry.

That is not to say that the essays themselves are not intelligent, lucid

and useful. John Gage's essay on Rothko's colour provides some new thinking on the artist. Specifically, Gage's recognition of the influence of Max Doerner as opposed to the general aesthetics of the Wilhelm Ostwald colour wheel, which Rothko disparaged as "Bauhaus ideology", is illuminating. Doerner's emphasis on the internal life of colour, of the blending of thin colour, of the mixing of white, can be found in Rothko. So, too, can the use of colour harmonies that are subjective and not standardised. The essay suffers, however, because these observations often float away as a formal discussion failing to recognise and add to their meaningfulness for Rothko. Comments that Rothko drew from Pompeian wall painting only after a trip to Europe in 1959 and that he was interested in Freudian psychoanalysis without acknowledgement of his and his colleagues' larger interest in Jungian ideas in the 1940s need more grounding and revision. It is not that Gage's essay is wrong, only that more can be said of the relationship of Rothko's colour to his ideas.

Barbara Novak's and Brian O'Doherty's essay follows the same pattern. O'Doherty was one of the best observers of Rothko's work in the 1960s and this essay on the artist's "Dark Painting" continues his examination of Rothko's general philosophising and its relationship to his form. Again, this line of inquiry is its strength and its weakness.

Mark Rothko's early masterpiece, 'Entrance to Subway', 1938

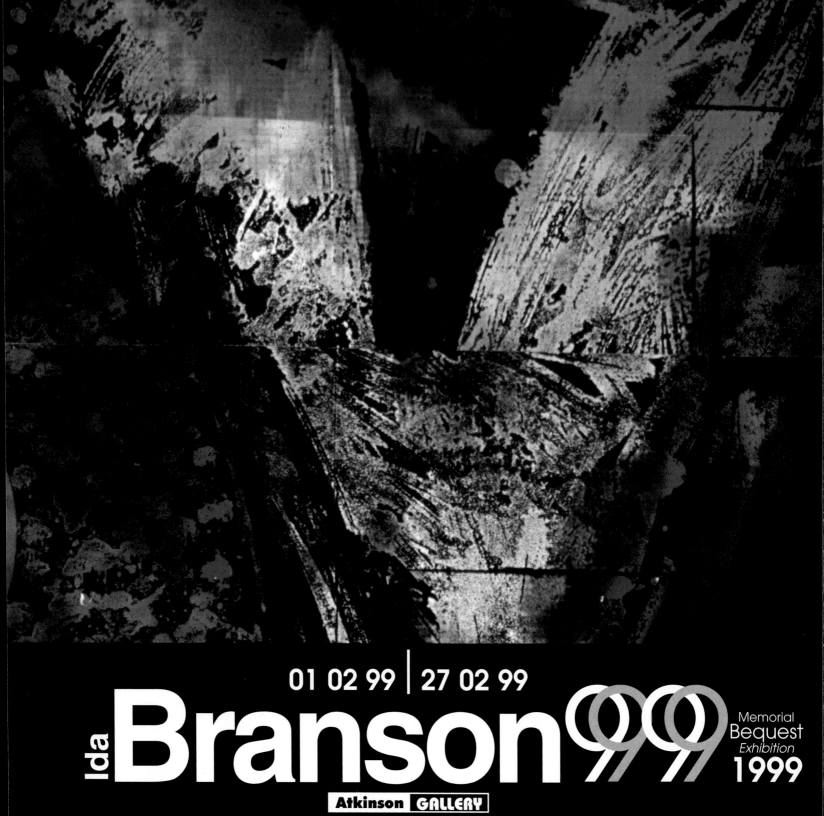

M.A. AND OTHER POSTGRADUATES' WORK

01 02 99 | 27 02 99

Ida Branson 99 Memorial Bequest Exhibition 1999

Atkinson GALLERY

For further information about the Millfield Art Projects please contact Len Green, Director of Art, Millfield, STREET,
Somerset BA16 OYD. Tel: 01458 442291, Fax: 01458 447276. Millfield is situated 10 miles off the A303 in Street, Somerset.

Insight

O'Doherty knew Rothko personally and his essay fuses acute insight into the general nature of the works with recorded comments by the artist. But much more is known since the 1960s and more can be said – both about the late paintings and Rothko's thought.

The only essay that engages with the early work is Weiss's. He attempts to make a continuity between the space in the early city and subway paintings and that in the later abstract, possibly sublime and existential work. While the sources for much of this essay remain unacknowledged again (Anfam for the city, myself for the architectural and expressive qualities of the sublime), it is an intelligent piece, suggesting a continuity in the idea of expressive space in Rothko's art. Rothko enveloped the protagonists in his early work in culturally significant architectural frames, and then surrounded the viewer more directly through pictorial effect in his later work. This envelopment by cultural frame and effect reflects his roots in the environmentalism of the 1930s, where the individual was recognised to be a product of his mental and spiritual, as well as his social and economic, environment. Weiss's essay embroiders this theme, although its roots in the 1930s are undiscussed.

Additional essays make further contributions. One by conservator Carol Mancusi-Ungaro continues her discerning work on Rothko's techniques and surfaces, while another investigates the impact and relevance of Rothko on contemporary artists such as Ellsworth Kelly, Brice Marden, George Segal and others.

What is missing in the catalogue and in the show is serious mention of the contribution of the history and culture of the time to the artist's formative ideas. The catalogue especially fails to convey and contribute much to the richness of the milieu from which Rothko came, so that his art and thought are presented as more idiosyncratic and personal than they were. That his art is mostly subjective and individualist reflects the viewpoint of the 1950s when the public address and framework of the Abstract Expressionists was lost upon the new youthful generation, the New York School and its new critics. This show and catalogue have left it to others to continue to correct this distortion.

BOOK

Monet in the 20th Century
Edited by Paul Hayes Tucker et al
Yale University Press, £30
Reviewed by Kathleen Adler

The first question that this book/catalogue of a major exhibition at the Museum of Fine Arts, Boston, and the Royal Academy of Arts, London, provokes is: "Why another Monet exhibition?" Such shows are the staple of museums around the world, the public appetite for the work of Monet seemingly insatiable. But a quick glance at the publication persuades one that market forces are not the sole reason by any means for undertaking this project.

The last 25 years of Monet's career as a painter, although obviously addressed in several previous exhibitions, have never been as thoroughly examined as here, and it is only in the opening essay of the book, John House's "Monet: The Last Impressionist?", that links back to the early years of Impressionism are made. In the other sections, it is Monet's production after the turn of the century, and the reception his work was accorded in France in the years immediately after his death and in the United States in the 1950s, that are the focus of discussion.

House questions whether Monet abandoned his aims of the "high Impressionist years of the 1870s", or whether he redefined them, remaining, in the end, faithful to "the basic tenets of Impressionist vision". His emphasis on Monet's desire for unity and for capturing the so-called *enveloppe* – the distinctive atmosphere and light of a motif – leads him to opt for the second of these possibilities, that the 'Grandes Décorations', the great waterlily paintings, are the culmination of a process begun far earlier in Monet's long career. He emphasises the importance of that concept of *sensations* so often discussed in the literature on Cézanne, the expression of his personal experience.

Paul Tucker, in his long essay "The Revolution in the Garden: Monet in the Twentieth Century", delves deeper into the political and social background against which he believes the prodigious production of

Monet's last years, some 450 paintings, must be seen. He sees the years of the Dreyfus Affair in the late 1890s, when France was deeply split politically, as affecting Monet to the point where his belief in the French nation could no longer be sustained, where he needed to redefine the meaning of his work. Tucker's view, therefore, is opposed to that of House, since although he acknowledges a continuum between the works of the twentieth century and the earlier Impressionist paintings, he insists that the political events of the day make it essential to see the later paintings as different in meaning from the earlier ones. So he interprets one of the 1889 series of views of the Creuse Valley, 'Study of Rocks (Le Bloc)', (from the Queen Mother's collection) as analogous to his friend the politician Georges Clemenceau's "valiant stand against the forces of hate and evil that had so riddled their beloved France".

In addition to addressing in considerable detail the issue of whether Monet's many decades of production should be seen as a continuum or broken up into very distinctive phases, the publication examines at least three of the great clichés of Monet scholarship: the impact of Turner on his work; the effect of his deteriorating eyesight on his painting; and the hoary question of his influence on avant-garde painting in New York in the 1950s.

Turner is cited as an influence on Impressionism almost as a matter of course in the huge literature on the subject, but the connection is seldom explored in detail. Tucker asserts that Monet was acutely conscious of Turner's wish to be compared with Claude, and was setting up the same direct confrontation. The impact of Monet's deteriorating vision and problems of colour perception which followed his cataract operations in 1923 are also discussed by Tucker, who refutes the idea that the artist could no longer see well enough to paint, although the colour balance of pre- and post-operative paintings may be different. But the most significant contribution that this important book makes to Monet studies is in its assessment of his position in the art worlds of Paris and New York after his death. Romy Golan's essay, "Oceanic Sensations: Monet's 'Grandes Décorations' and Mural Painting in France from 1927 to

Claude Monet, 'The Japanese Bridge', 1919-1924

1952", traces the changing fortunes of the waterlily paintings unveiled in the Orangerie in Paris in May 1927, disregarded and allowed to deteriorate from the date of their installation until 1952. The 'Décorations', as Golan shows, were out of step with the *rappel à l'ordre* of the 1920s, their individuality out of phase even with the revival of mural painting of the 1930s. The sense that the 'Grandes Décorations' conveyed a lonely, existential struggle – the nemesis of the works in the pre-war years – became their strength in the post-war period, when they could be seen as "one of the peaks of French genius".

In New York, the 1950s marked a crescendo of interest in Monet's late works, with Clement Greenberg prescribing how they might be seen. In Greenberg's view, Monet was a solver of pictorial problems, who had not fully understood the "abstract" qualities of his late work, which became an important link between Impressionism and the Abstract Expressionism of Pollock, Newman, Guston and others. The spread from *Life*, reproduced on page 107, makes abundantly clear the visual links that were seen to exist between Monet's late paintings and American Abstract Expressionism, while the irritating details of enlarged (but meaningless) brush strokes interspersed throughout this volume are no doubt intended to keep reminding us of Monet's "abstract" qualities.

The catalogue section of the book consists of excellent colour plates with minimal information, but this information is of course available in the four-volume reprint of Daniel Wildenstein's catalogue *raisonné* of the artist. The essays take Monet studies into new areas. The publication is much to be welcomed, as the exhibition at the Royal Academy surely will be.

Who needs 'art for everyone'?

According to the chairman of the Arts Council, art is élitist and needs to reach a wider audience. Andrew Brighton disagrees vehemently

Imagine that the Department of Education and Employment determined that *Sun* and *Mirror* readers, the unemployed and ethnic minorities were linguistically deprived and should be encouraged to have French lessons. Future funding of some university French departments and a substantial tranche of Lottery money available to others becomes dependent on their ability to attract these audiences. To further these aims, it is required that they be flexible and teach Franglais.

This may sound improbable, but it is a pretty good analogy for the implications of Arts Council chairman Gerry Robinson's "An Arts Council for the Future" speech given at the Royal Society of Arts. Its implications for modern and contemporary visual arts should be examined. The policies he has declared for his "new era for the arts" set the priorities for the Council and the Regional Arts Board's temporary exhibition venues and visual arts schemes. They also set the requirements for the Lottery funds the Council distributes. Applicants in England, including non-Arts Council supported museums and galleries, will have to adhere to these criteria.

The key phrase is "Art for Everyone". Two requirements emerge. Firstly, arts organisations should reach out not just to larger but also "new" audiences. Galleries and museums will be obliged to increase the resources, time and space devoted to them. They must be seen to bring in more members of social and ethnic groups statistically under-represented at arts events. The arts should be ashamed of their predominantly white, middle-class audiences and Robinson uses "élite" as a term of disparagement. Secondly, the kinds of art offered must be "flexible" to attract these non-attendees.

Gerry Robinson quotes George Steiner's charge of "vengeful philistinism" against our political masters and their minions. He says the flaw in Steiner's argument "is his suggestion that high art and popular art are somehow foes that cannot co-exist". They do co-exist, but not in the same institutions. The forms of marketing and display and cultures of reception are radically different. In 1980, a Mintel survey estimated the value of UK retail sales of reproductions and limited edition prints to be between £35 million and £100 million. Purchases were made by all social classifications (ABs to Es) from market stalls and Boots as well as galleries. In a survey I did a couple of years earlier I estimated the sales of galleries dealing in contemporary art including original works at around £8 million. In other words, the uses of images are widely spread throughout society and are not limited to artefacts available in specialist galleries.

Arguably Dr Colin Painter has published the most informative research on the uses of images and objects across the social spectrum in this country. He visited a whole range of homes and discussed with the occupants what they had on their walls. He found that virtually every home had non-utilitarian artefacts on display, but did their owners consider them to be art? Middle-class people tended to nominate certain objects, such as paintings and reproductions, as art. Whereas the tendency in working-class homes was to have more various objects and images and to value them for their association with friends and relatives. To conceptualise these things as art was irrelevant; it was like being asked to speak a foreign language. Painter did not see working-class people as visually deprived and in need of a visit from an art evangelist.

Somewhere Wittgenstein said that to understand an aesthetic judgment is to understand a whole form of life. Clearly, people from many forms of life are making aesthetic judgments, but not all of them think of these as judgments about art. Is then the demand for "Art for Everyone" a demand that everyone should have, or affect to have, the same form of life?

We have diverse sub-cultures of images, of which modern art is one. It is, however, the most serious. It has an academic and critical literature. Robinson wishes to build into public funding the erosion of the particular cultures of each art. He asserts: "Traditional artforms are hardy and capable of innovation and reinvention; but flexibility has always characterised the arts and artists." Strange: in my experience, a necessary obstinacy characterises most artists. He goes on: "In the past the Arts Council has tended to distribute its budget largely according to artform. Perhaps it is time now for a funding system better adapted to that flexibility."

To propose that the kinds of modern and contemporary art collected and displayed by all the publicly supported galleries should be "flexible" to attract those otherwise uninterested in what they exhibit is to strike at the specific character of the museums and galleries and their audiences. Modern art is not a chronological label; it refers to a self-conscious tradition of art practice and debate in which what constitutes art and value are contested. This tradition values not only the pleasures of art; it values anxiety, doubt, difficulty and thinking. It is a foe of the habitual certainties of our collective culture. Modern art has, however, courted, plundered and praised popular culture when it has shared its dissenting energies. This culture of art has a self-electing audience which is now in its millions, and it is a growing one.

The most salient predictor for arts audiences is neither wealth nor income, it is education. This was the finding, for instance, of Dimaggio and Useem in their survey of surveys of art audiences in the US, where museums and galleries are not free and levels of public subsidy are lower than in Europe. It is the relatively highly educated – teachers, academics and professionals – who constitute the core of regular arts consumers.

Why is there a growing audience for modern and contemporary art, for that tradition of the new and the questioning? One answer lies in returning to Wittgenstein's assertion that aesthetic judgments have their origin in forms of life. I suggest that the character of their work determines the sensibilities of intellectual workers. The minds of people who organise people, data, concepts, knowledge, ideas or images, communicating and arguing, are shaped in part by what they do. Reflexivity, criticality, what the sociologist Alvin Gouldner called the "Culture of Critical Discourse", finds itself both valued and questioned. As our economy is increasingly knowledge- and communications-based, these forms of professional life are shared by a growing number of people from different social and ethnic backgrounds. Some of these may choose to do French lessons, but they will not want to learn Franglais.

As anybody who attends music, theatre and visual arts events knows, the audiences differ in age, style and ethnic mix. Is Robinson guilty of social stereotyping? The middle-class is not a homogeneous stratum. Diverse and conflicting values, beliefs, cultural pleasures and expectations resist the homogenising instincts of the state. The differences between the broadsheet newspapers are a symptom of an even more complex range of ideologies and ways of life. Are we really that contemptible?

A. KRAUZE

ANDRZEJ KRAUZE